SOCIALI

HUTCHINSON'S UNIVERSITY LIBRARY
POLITICS

EDITOR:

PROFESSOR G. D. H. COLE

*Chichele Professor of Social and Political Theory
in the University of Oxford*

SOCIALISM
A SHORT HISTORY

by

NORMAN MACKENZIE

HUTCHINSON'S UNIVERSITY LIBRARY

1949

11 Stratford Place, London, W.1

New York *Melbourne* *Sydney* *Cape Town*

THIS VOLUME IS NUMBER 36 IN
HUTCHINSON'S UNIVERSITY LIBRARY

FOR
JOHN OAKLEY
Drongen : May, 1944

*Printed in Great Britain
by The Anchor Press, Ltd.,
Tiptree, Essex*

CONTENTS

FOREWORD

BOTH the philosophy of socialism and the movements which have sprung from it have long and complex histories. To deal with either properly the reader must turn to more elaborate and specialized studies, of which a selection is recommended at the end of this book. In this outline history, however, I have sought to trace both the political ideas and their associated movements from their origins to our own time, so that this volume may serve as an introduction or, in a sense, as a guide-book to the milestones that mark the road socialism has travelled.

Naturally I have had to express opinions and make judgments. Without doubt these are open to criticism. But I have tried to make this book factually accurate and, wherever differences of opinion are important, fairly to state opposing views. I believe free comment is vital to a free society. If this book helps to stimulate intelligent criticism or debate it will have made its contribution. Those who may disagree with my conclusions or who may wish to check them against standard authorities will find ample material in the books I suggest for further reading.

N. M.

CHAPTER I

THE SOCIALIST CHALLENGE

In July 1945 the British electorate sent a Labour majority to Parliament. For the first time in our history a party based upon a democratic socialist programme was returned to office and to power. Before 1914 the Labour Party was little more than a radical offshoot from the Liberals; after 1918 it became the official Opposition at Westminster, and formed two minority administrations, each of which had a short and difficult life. Within forty years of its foundation the Labour Party had risen from its humble and unpretentious beginning to the foremost place in British politics.

When Mr. Attlee became Prime Minister it was an event of great importance. Until the rise of the Labour Party, British politics were largely a contest between two big parties which both agreed that whatever else the State might do, it should interfere as little as possible with the conduct of the nation's economic affairs. There were major differences between the Liberals and Conservatives, but both parties were, and remain, based on the assumption that capitalist enterprise is more efficient and desirable than public ownership or control of industry and commerce.

The Labour Party, on the other hand, has sought to reconstruct the whole basis of our society by transferring the direction of a large part of our economy from individuals to the State. When Labour formed a majority Government, therefore, the British people were faced with the prospect of moving, for a time at least, in a socialist direction. Though the initial stages of the Labour Government's policy did not involve any drastic changes in our way of life, they were clearly a departure from the familiar and traditional economic pattern. Capitalist ownership might still be predominant in most industries and trades, but the successful completion of Labour's long-term plans would ensure that certain important sectors of the economy—fuel, transport,

9

perhaps steel—would pass under State ownership, while the economy as a whole would be subject to a central control and direction.

Socialism may be denounced or supported, but it certainly cannot be ignored. Elections, it is true, are rarely fought on theoretical questions. People judge their governments by their ability to build enough houses, to prevent unemployment, and to ensure proper provision for the education of children and the care of the sick and old. But it is part of the Labour Party's case that these tasks can be carried out efficiently, in the modern world, only by conscious socialist planning of the nation's resources.

The opponents of socialism, however, insist that it will lead to bureaucracy, to administrative inefficiency, and even to the elimination of free political institutions. Thus, in choosing a Labour or a Tory candidate to represent them at Westminster, electors today are playing a part in a far bigger drama than the old contest of Liberal and Conservative.

It is a commonplace today to remark that we live in a revolutionary age, when the established moral values are losing their hold; when religions are replaced by new ideologies; and when it is impossible to provide adequate food, shelter and clothing for millions, in spite of the fact that machinery has endowed man with an unprecedented productive capacity.

There have been other periods like this in history. Capitalism itself developed only after a long and bloody struggle against the restrictive power of medieval society. In its time, as socialists admit, it was an immense revolutionary force, which produced new wealth, fresh economic methods and political institutions, different habits and a changed attitude to life. But socialists also argue that, in turn, capitalist technique has outlived its usefulness and has become a brake upon man's progress towards a fuller and more generous existence. They say that the recurrent economic crises are preventable, that socialism can eliminate the poverty, ill-health and lack of opportunity which has been the lot of so many men and women. They believe that the working-class, by whose labours the achievements of industrial capitalism were attained and who suffered most in the process, is capable of winning State power and carrying through the political and economic changes which are necessary to prevent our civilization collapsing in war and chaos.

In spite of the impressive support that socialism commands, there are some writers who contend that its vision of a more free and prosperous world is based upon an illusion. Hilaire Belloc, for instance, insisted that socialism in practice would plunge men into the misery of the Servile State. Professor Hayek, the eminent economist, whose *Road to Serfdom* was a best-seller, has said very much the same sort of thing in a more sophisticated way. In another popular book, *The Managerial Revolution*, the American, James Burnham, has argued that, irrespective of its desirability, socialism is impossible, since in modern industrial society power has, in fact, passed into the hands of the managers and technicians, the men who actually control production whether they are the nominal servants of the public or of shareholders.

Socialism, however, is a general term. One word, whose broad meaning is pretty generally understood, is also used indiscriminately to represent the outlook of a large number of groups whose philosophies and methods are by no means the same. No single phrase can cover all the variations in emphasis and principle. Socialism means different things to different men. There is nothing that better illustrates this point than the fact that a book published in the 'Twenties contained more than two hundred definitions of socialism by leading figures in British public life alone.

For some people socialism is primarily an attempt to establish a more moral society. Capitalism, they say, is based on a harsh and corrupting system of ethics, which makes a virtue of greed and selfishness. It must, therefore, be replaced by a society in which men regard each other as brothers and prefer co-operation to wasteful competition. For others, socialism is the most rational and efficient form of social organization, ensuring the best use of human and material resources. For the Marxists, especially, it is the only logical and possible step forward for humanity. On the one hand industrial capitalism is the cause of war, imperialism and economic chaos. On the other, by creating a working-class which is disciplined into organization by the factory system, it prepares the means for its own overthrow.

There are many reasons why men become socialists: there are many forms that socialism can take. In the last hundred and fifty years socialism has been forced to discard a large number of ideas, important enough in their day, which experience proved to be illusory or impracticable. Yet the central tradition has gone on growing, and at each new stage in its development, in the light of parallel changes in social structure, in scientific knowledge, and in the problems which faced the working-class movement, the doctrine has been refined and extended.

Since the Bolshevik Revolution in 1917 the Left has been divided into two main camps: the communists and social-democrats. Anarchism, which played an important role in the nineteenth century and in the less industrialized countries, has gradually been submerged. The communist parties, based firmly on a common doctrine and united under the central control of the Communist International—dissolved in 1943 but resurrected in the Communist Information Bureau—have always had a disciplined coherence which endowed them with greater strength than their numbers seemed to merit. But social democracy varies from one nation to another. The labour and socialist parties share a belief in the possibility of reforming the capitalist State from within, and have no faith in the value of violent action by the workers in order to seize political power. But they have more method than philosophy in common. Their members may base their socialism on Marx, Kant, Bernard Shaw, Rousseau, or the Bible, as they please. Most of·them have geared their organization and their activity to the requirements of the electoral system.

The rift between democratic socialists and communists has become wider in the post-war world. Though socialist parties have been swept into, or close to, power in a number of democracies, the communists now control Eastern Europe, as well as the Soviet Union and vast areas of China, and in other countries they are pressing hard for leadership of the working-class movements. Today the world is divided, not, as the early socialists expected, between the capitalists and the angry exploited masses, but between two rival centres of power. There are socialists in both camps: in the Eastern bloc are the communists and their allies, who insist that their road is the only road to real socialism and that the democratic socialists of the West are dupes of capitalism; and in the Western bloc the social-democrats retort that the Communist States are tyrannies, that in a choice between democracy—with all the faults that follow from capitalism—and one-party rule, though it may masquerade as socialism, they prefer democracy. Democratic socialism, as exemplified by our own Labour Party, now has few "illusions" about communism. Neither side trusts the other nor, at this moment, admits that it can achieve socialism. The opposing taunts, "Tyrant," "Traitor", are now heard between nations, not merely between factions on the Left.

It is against this background that the policy and actions of the Labour Party must be judged. They are but one aspect of an historical movement on a world scale which is still gathering momentum. No sensible person now suggests that socialism is the doctrine merely of malcontents. But it is still not generally realized that it grows inevitably out of our present social system, which is based upon capitalist enterprise in industry, commerce and agriculture.

This book is a short account of how all this has come about. It is an attempt to show the main landmarks on the road along which socialism has already travelled; for only this enables us to make a balanced assessment of its present strength and of the picture it presents of our world. For further details of the doctrines and movements here described the reader must look elsewhere. The economic history of the last two hundred years, without which the rise of socialism is unintelligible, is sketched merely in broad terms, for it is accessible in a score of popular books. This generation is squarely confronted with the socialist challenge. It is the purpose of this book concisely to explain its history and meaning.

CHAPTER II

THE BIRTH OF AN IDEA

WHERE does the history of socialism begin? Both the political doctrine and the mass labour organizations, in their familiar and modern form, are essentially the product of the nineteenth century. They began, early in the industrial age, as a protest against the misery of the factory system, which had disrupted the traditional pattern of economic activity, and as a means by which a growing and exploited working-class could defend itself against the hard, new masters, who demanded the maximum of effort in return for the least possible reward. Socialism grew to maturity as capitalist enterprise spread across the world, and the utopian schemes of the pioneers were discarded for a more elaborate indictment of the capitalist society, which seemed unable to prevent recurrent wars and financial crises. The second half of the nineteenth century was the great period in which rival groups thrashed out the main theoretical problems of socialism and laid the foundations of the mass movements we know today. In the last thirty years socialists have spent part of their time refining and extending doctrines whose basic principles were clearly established before 1914, and, for the rest, meeting the tactical difficulties that arose from their increasing strength and from the prospect, in a number of countries, that they would be called upon to accept the responsibilities of power.

But socialism, like other philosophies, owes a great deal to the past. Though, as a serious movement of social criticism and reform, it dates back barely a hundred and fifty years, its ancestry can be traced to some of the greatest figures in the cultural and political life of Europe. It is one aspect of the civilized tradition that started in ancient Greece and Rome. It has inherited the radical interpretation of Christianity. Continental socialism, in part, sprang from the philosophy of Hegel. Under the different conditions, the old utilitarian, Jeremy Bentham, left an abiding mark on the English labour movement which grew up after his death in 1832. Rousseau, too, Tom Paine and others who led the democratic assault on privilege and autocracy, are now acclaimed as men who marked out the road that socialism was later to follow.

There is nothing new in the idea that misery and injustice are the result of the division of society into rich and poor. In European literature, up to the dawn of the machine era, there was a recurring belief in a lost golden age when, before the advent of civilization with its attendant vices of poverty and privilege, men lived a simple pastoral life, holding all things in common. Socialism, at least as much as any other contemporary doctrine, is the heir to that intermingling of Greek philosophy, Roman law and Christian religion on which the democratic tradition rests. In early socialist speculation there are frequent appeals to antiquity. Mably, the French philosopher of the eighteenth century, who provided most of the intellectual inspiration for the abortive communist revolt led by Babeuf in the last stages of the French Revolution, drew heavily upon Plato and Lycurgus of Sparta. The Christian teachings, even the communal life of the early Christians themselves, powerfully influenced the peasant revolts at the close of the Middle Ages, the extreme Left-wing groups in the English Civil War, and, more recently, some of the chief founders of the Labour Party in Britain.

Socialism today is not only a vision of what life could be like in a rational society; it is also a political technique. Most socialists regard the working-class as the social group which presses most consistently for the limitation of the abuses of capitalism and its eventual overthrow. To accomplish this task, organization is necessary. Socialist parties work within the framework of the capitalist State to secure, either by reform or revolution, the political power they require to shape both the institutions and economic structure of society to their ends.

Before the rise of modern industry, with its immense productive capacities, and the emergence of an organized working-class seeking to transfer the ownership and control of production from private to public hands, socialism, as we know it, was an impossibility. There were many critics in the past who showed a penetrating insight into the causes of distress, injustice and discontent. Some of them went further and envisaged the broad outlines of a more harmonious and prosperous world. But the resources, the technical development and political methods of achieving it were lacking, and they had to fall back on remedies which were doomed from the start to failure.

All the same, their work was not fruitless. They kept the socialist tradition alive until the day when it became something more than a vision. They desired fraternity and equality among men; they insisted that the unequal distribution of wealth and power was the origin of misery and corruption; and they dreamed of a regenerated society where men, no longer divided into masters and servants, would co-operate for the common good.

By general consent the most remarkable of these pioneers was Sir Thomas More. His *Utopia*, published in 1516, is the greatest of all social fantasies. Unlike many similar works, it was not constructed out of abstract ideas, nor does it glance back to a happy pastoral society lost in the shadows of history. More was one of the foremost statesmen of his age, a man of great personal integrity and intellectual ability. Much of his *Utopia* is devoted to a description of England at the beginning of the sixteenth century, when the breakdown of the static medieval economy was raising new and unprecedented problems. Great fortunes were being made in commerce, especially in the developing wool trade, while the peasantry were being driven from the land and their places taken by the more profitable sheep. Through the mouth of a Portuguese explorer, Raphael Hythloday, More tells the story of the island of Utopia as a contrast to the state of England, where private property, the exclusion of the many from the means of life for the benefit of the few, is the root of evil. "Where possessions are private, where money is the measure of all things," says Hythloday, "it is hard and almost impossible that the commonwealth should have just government and enjoy prosperity."

But in Utopia, where the citizens pool the products of their labour and draw what they need from the common storehouse, there is peace and security. Men under communism have neither need nor desire for personal wealth to ensure their comfort and freedom from oppression. The people of Utopia, unlike the unhappy English, understand that the scramble for riches is the root of ambition, of civil strife, of wars, even of the decay of nations. *Utopia* is probably the finest work produced by any of the primitive communist writers. Unlike most of them, More saw that a workable communist system must control production as well as ensure an equal distribution of goods. Though he shared their inability to suggest any really practical way of accomplishing the transition to the ideal community, none of them rivalled him in scope or clarity of description. His *Utopia* has survived, to our own time, as a brilliant picture of the life that men both could and ought to live.

For more than a hundred years before the publication of More's remarkable book there had been an undercurrent of discontent among the English peasantry, which at times broke out into open revolt. Heresy, encouraged by itinerant friars, was widespread. The peasants, increasingly divorced from the land, lacking any social rights, sought the restitution of ancient Christian equality and the abolition of the pomp and splendour of contemporary Catholicism. It was but a short step for them to demand the elimination of civil privilege and the sharing of all property. In the Peasant Revolt of 1381, the priest, John Ball, preached the brotherhood of men, created equal by nature and deprived of their rights by lords, judges and lawyers. There was a similar outbreak led by Jack Cade in 1449.

On the Continent, like heresies led to peasant wars. Mystical sects, such as the Bohemian Taborites and Münzer in Germany, managed to dominate large districts for years. Even after their violent suppression their ideas lingered on in Europe. In those days, it must be remembered, all thought was cast in the religious mould of the Catholic Church. Social discontent could only become articulate as a heresy, which was then bitterly attacked by the combined efforts of the princes and the Church. Yet, in spite of brutality and bloodshed, these plebeian heresies flourished among the peasants and among the poorer townsmen, keeping alive the early Christian doctrine that private property was sinful and an obstacle to salvation. The belief also gained ground that men had a right to an equal share of the wealth that they produced.

B

By the beginning of the English Civil War, in 1642, Puritanism, which had begun as a heresy, had taken hold among the wealthy commercial class in the towns. It was a democratic doctrine, developed in the struggle against an obsolete monarchy and a corrupt Church. Throughout this revolutionary period it served as a suitable ideology for a merchant capitalism which was successfully destroying the political, economic and religious fetters that handicapped the expansion of trade, the easy and profitable circulation of capital and the establishment of a representative, if at that time limited, democracy. But in times of social upheaval more radical ideas are always brought to the fore. By 1648 the rank-and-file of the Parliamentary armies had swung over to support the Levellers, who sought to carry the new democratic ideas to their logical conclusion, to attack all privilege, and to claim the earth as the natural inheritance of all men. The Levellers concentrated upon political reform: there is an implicit socialism in their doctrine, but it is never stated. Still couching their philosophy in religious language, they found their golden age in Saxon England, before the Norman Conquest had placed a privileged and alien hierarchy in power and driven its rightful owners from their communal enjoyment of the soil of England.

This idea was expressed even more forcibly by Gerard Winstanley, the leader of a small group known as the Diggers. Unlike the Levellers, they had little faith in political action of the normal kind and they were much more precise about the society they wished to set up immediately in England. Declaring that the Civil War had been fought to restore their rights to the people of England, in April 1649 Winstanley and some of his followers began to dig the common at St. George's Hill, Weybridge. They were later driven off by a troop of cavalry. Winstanley then turned writer and worked out a doctrine to justify his action. In some remarkable passages he anticipates much that figures prominently in later socialism. Society, he said, is divided into warring classes. Political struggles are a reflection of property interests. Co-operative work and collective possession must one day replace hired labour and private ownership if men are to enjoy freedom, happiness and prosperity.

Winstanley's experiment failed, inevitably. Though, for another two hundred years, no one in England produced a more brilliant or realistic socialist analysis, he had little influence upon his own or subsequent generations. Yet, indirectly, he is linked to the modern socialist movement. Some of his ideas were embodied in a book, written by John Bellers in 1696, called *The College of Industry*, which advocated a system of co-operative and self-supporting communities. Many years afterwards a copy of this book fell into the hands of Robert Owen, the factory owner, who is generally regarded as the father of the early-nineteenth-century socialist and co-operative moments in Britain. In acknowledging his debt to Bellers, as he did, Owen was also paying a tribute to Winstanley.

There are important similarities between the Civil War in England and the French Revolution. In the same way the struggle against feudalism was at first undertaken by the moderate middle-class parties, which, under the strain of war and social dislocation, were increasingly challenged by more extreme groups, composed partly of the poor and propertyless. But these events in France took place more than a hundred years later and were influenced by the political thought and experience of those intervening years.

In England, at the end of the revolutionary upheaval, there appeared the mystic agrarian reformer Winstanley. In France the final stages of the Revolution threw up Babeuf and his militant communist conspiracy.

Before Babeuf, who stands at the divide between primitive and modern socialism, there are a few French writers who can justly be associated with the socialist tradition. Two of them, Mably and Morelly, both widely read in their own day, were advocates of a full, if fantastic, communism, and they undoubtedly had a considerable influence upon Babeuf. Rousseau, the most influential of all the French philosophers, certainly cannot be called a socialist. But his passionate attacks on wealth, his denunciations of the corrupting environment of society, his eulogy of equality and his insistence that primitive men had once held all things in common, left their mark on Jacobins like Marat and Robespierre, and on groups that stood even further to the Left.

After the fall of Robespierre it was clear that the individualist peasant and the speculator had profited most from the sacrifices of the Revolution. Babeuf, and the other remarkable men associated with him in the "Conspiracy of the Equals", sought to carry the struggle a stage further. Whereas most primitive socialists had contented themselves with charting the details of a new society—and Babeuf himself worked out the main features of his communist State with some care—they had failed to evolve a practicable means of winning and maintaining power to accomplish the transition. Babeuf, for the first time, produced a revolutionary technique. He did this with such skill that the methods of the conspirators have provided the basis of revolutionary socialist strategy ever since. They appealed directly to the Parisian working-class; they developed an elaborate propaganda machine; they formed secret cells in the army and the police. Since the rich will never voluntarily surrender their power, they said, it must be taken from them by force.

After the success of the revolt, a dictatorship is necessary for the period of transition to communist democracy, but work will be provided for all, there will be free medical services and education, the prison system will be reformed and the aged will receive State pensions. The individual will fulfil himself in the service of the whole community. Private property will be abolished, since it is an incitement to civil war and prevents men sharing equally in wealth and happiness.

There is much in the outlook of the conspirators that reveals how far they were truly forerunners of modern socialist thought. Their revolt failed and Babeuf himself died on the guillotine. But they left an enduring legacy. One of them, Buonarroti, later wrote the history of the conspiracy, after spending thirty years working with men who played a leading part in the foundation of socialist groups in France, Britain, Belgium and Germany. Babeuf brought something new to socialism. He, more than anyone else, stands at the beginning of the road that led to Lenin and the Bolshevik Revolution of 1917. He was the first socialist of any importance to declare that working-class power could be won only by a revolution as carefully prepared as a military operation.

Though the Napoleonic Empire placed the rich and the privileged in power again, it did not restore the old régime. France was no longer a feudal country. The speculator had replaced the aristocratic landlord; the serf had been turned into a free peasant. Capitalist social relationships were spreading fast. Yet the intense political experience of the Revolution could not easily be forgotten. Socialist ideas were no longer an abstract doctrine. Men had learnt that the State might be used to abolish privilege, to direct production and control distribution, to give reward according to need, to sustain the interests of the poor against the greed and exploitation of the rich.

France, at this time, seemed to have lost its sense of political direction. The old régime had vanished: the new age of industry and commerce was scarcely born. Henri de Saint-Simon believed that he had an answer. Of aristocratic origins, he had fought in the American War of Independence and had seen for himself the birth of a new democratic republic, based on the hard work of merchants and farmers. Where, he asked, were men to find the sources of a political and spiritual power which could replace all that had been lost with the overthrow of feudalism? They should embrace a new religion that would replace the orthodox Christianity, which had completed its historic mission. They should behave as brothers, they should subordinate everything to the effort "to ameliorate as promptly and as quickly as possible the moral and physical existence of the most numerous class".

This idea that the proper function of the State is to ensure the welfare of the masses was Saint-Simon's greatest contribution to political thought, though he himself was no socialist in the modern sense. He believed in the retention of privilege and private property, as long as both status and wealth were the reward of hard work of value to the community. He thought all men should be given equal opportunities in life, but he was willing to concede the capitalist his profits if he understood that property also entailed social responsibilities. There is much, in fact, in his philosophy which can be interpreted as an intelligent anticipation of the practices of private enterprise in an industrial society, even of the corporate State. But, on the other hand, by a slight change in emphasis, part of his doctrine was easily turned into a socialist critique of capitalism.

Later in the nineteenth century Marxism was to take from him the thesis that one day political government would be replaced by the expert administration of production and distribution, though, for Marx and Engels, that day would come only when the victory of full communism had eliminated the need for the State as an instrument of class rule. Saint-Simon, moreover, was the first social philosopher to relate the growth of science and the technical revolution which proceeded from it to form a theory of historical development which could explain, coherently, the course of man and society through the ages. In this, too, he can be said to anticipate Marx and Engels.

Besides Saint-Simon there was another eccentric Frenchman who is now regarded as one of the socialist pioneers. Charles Fourier was also far from being a consistent or coherent socialist. He had a passion for completing his pictures of social organization down to the last comma. Though his imagination often ran riot in the universe as well as on this planet, to a degree which is both baffling and amusing, he had a considerable influence for many years after his death in 1837. Commerce, he said, made virtue less lucrative than vice. Every individual is at war with the interests of the community in his search for personal wealth. This unnecessary competition produces only waste and parasitism—a conclusion that evoked a wide response in France. If work is to be made pleasant and attractive, if men are to be happy, they must establish co-operative settlements—to which he gave the name of phalanxes—in which there would be an opportunity for everyone to find employment which would be both lucrative and suitable for the creative expression of personality. Fourier did not desire a barrack-room equality within his phalanx. On the contrary, wealth would be no sin provided it was achieved by co-operative means. But every individual would be guaranteed a minimum standard of life.

Fourier, typically, worked out the last administrative and constructional details of his phalanxes. Stripped of its obvious absurdities, his idea was sufficiently attractive to inspire a number of experiments. But the fate of the colonies founded on Fourier's model in both Europe and America was a demonstration of the futility of trying to change the structure of society by example. In the early nineteenth century success went to the men who were transforming the face of the world by the development of industry and commerce, not to those who spent their energies in the formation of idyllic self-supporting communities.

The followers of Saint-Simon did not waste their strength in the fashion of many energetic Fourierists. In spite of internal quarrels and the difficulties into which the Saint-Simonian school fell when its more extreme members tried to carry out the moral and religious precepts of their master, it produced a flood of propaganda aimed, with some accuracy, at the abuses consequent upon the development of industrial capitalism. It attacked inheritance and denounced exploitation; it insisted that the State should eventually own the land and the factories, and direct production in the interests of the community as a whole. Its teachings, in a simplified form, became associated with the discontent among the growing working-class of France. Its enthusiasm for vast public works found an echo in later French socialism. Some of the Saint-Simonians, who were a brilliant group of young men, afterwards became prominent business men and engineers who were largely responsible, among other achievements, for the building of the French railway system and the Suez Canal.

But by 1830 new forces were at work. The "utopian socialists", as they were later and finally classified by Marx and Engels in the *Communist Manifesto*, had laid the groundwork for their successors in the age of industry and had little more to say or do. In their day they were men of remarkable, though erratic, insight. They arose in a period of transition. They never had to face the problems of a highly-organized industrial system.

The modern working-class movement had not then developed, and they had no real idea of how a new social order could be set up. They appealed to humanity as a whole to be guided by their rational doctrine and, lacking any adequate sense of the pattern of historical development, did not understand that a ruling class does not voluntarily relinquish its power. They believed that it was only necessary for a man of genius to appear and proclaim the need for a new and regenerated society for all men to realize that their prosperity and happiness depended on the acceptance of his doctrine. Yet, for all their weaknesses, these men were the pioneers of modern socialism. Most of them devoted their lives to the struggle to free their fellow men from want, misery and oppression. More than that, in their time, they could not do.

CHAPTER III

OWEN AND THE CHARTISTS

In the first half of the nineteenth century the foundations of modern industry and socialism were firmly laid in Great Britain. On the Continent the working-class emerged as an important and independent political force only during the revolutions in 1848. But by that time the British proletariat had already created its own mass party and trade union organizations, experimented with co-operative enterprises, and, from a variety of teachers, learnt the essentials of socialism. While Britain was leading the world in the development of the industrial capitalist system, the workers were trying out in an embryonic form many of the methods and ideas which later were embodied in classical socialist theory.

There were propertyless wage-earners, with trade clubs to defend their interests, for a long time before the discovery of steam power and the other mechanical inventions which revolutionized industrial technique. But, in the absence of the factory system on a national scale, the strikes and protests of these workers were limited to particular areas or specific grievances; they could not possess either a sense of common purpose or the capacity for large-scale organization in their own interest.

Nevertheless, in the bigger towns in the woollen and mining industries a growing number of artisans and workers were caught up in the democratic agitation for the reform of the corrupt Parliamentary system. The London masses were brought into action by the struggle between their champion, John Wilkes, and the House of Commons, which refused to seat him. But until after the end of the Napoleonic Wars the initiative was taken by the skilled craftsmen, rather than by the misery-ridden miners and operatives.

It was the artisans who had formed the London Corresponding Society and similar groups in Manchester, Sheffield and

25

other towns. These were the first definitely political bodies of working-men. They were content, on the whole, to act under the leadership of the middle-class reform movement, but before long they also became the spokesmen of the larger and less articulate class of workers which lacked either their education or their income.

The French Revolution was a great stimulant to the democrats in Britain. Its ideas were spread throughout the country by Tom Paine, Thomas Hardy and other agitators. Demands for universal suffrage, for annual Parliaments, even for a republic, increased rapidly. But the movement was crushed before it achieved anything substantial. The network of corresponding societies was broken up by a series of treason trials after 1793. Many of the middle-class reformers were terrified into desertion by Pitt's campaign of repression and by the ruthlessness of Jacobin policy in France. Later, the naval mutinies at the Nore and Spithead, and the rebellion of the United Irishmen, provided a further scare for the middle-classes.

It was not merely political activity that was suppressed. The Combination Acts of 1799 and 1800 made all trade combinations illegal, though these laws were applied with a severity that varied from year to year and from one place to another, according to the strength of working-class discontent. But, under the pressure of war, industry was growing rapidly and trade unionism carried on an underground struggle among the workers, whose numbers increased every year.

The end of the Napoleonic Wars marked the start of a new phase in the reform movement. The workers, faced with widespread unemployment, again rallied behind the middle-class demand for a radical change in the British Constitution. The oligarchic Government of the time, in spite of new legislation and persecution—such as the Six Acts and the infamous massacre at St. Peter's Fields ("Peterloo") in 1819—found that the business men and the industrialists were not prepared to join in the suppression of working-class organizations which supported their campaign. The French menace was over, and the middle-classes were no longer satisfied to be ruled by an oligarchy which refused to admit them to their proper share of political power and restricted the growth of commerce and industry.

The face of Britain was changing fast. Between 1770 and 1820 more than five million acres of the common land had been expropriated by the richer landowners by the Enclosure Acts. The peasantry, driven from the soil, moved into the new towns like Manchester, where they could find work in the factories and mills. Men, women and children worked more than fourteen hours a day for little more than a bare sub-sistence wage and slept at nights in filthy hovels which were the breeding-ground of cholera and other diseases. They lived and died like animals and their masters grew wealthy on their misery. Naturally, many of them struck out blindly in self-defence. The ruined handloom-weavers tried to smash the new machines that they believed had caused their misery. But these sporadic revolts were always crushed.

Masses of the workers took part in the agitation which at last secured the Reform Act of 1832 and thereby served their political apprenticeship. The Combination Acts were repealed in 1824 and trade unions were once more able to operate openly. For the time, however, political rather than industrial action seemed the best means of securing a general improvement in the conditions of the working-class. As the Tory wing of the oligarchy could not be overthrown by violence, the Whigs, as the only other effective group in Parliament, had to carry through the long-overdue reforms. Under pressure from the commercial and industrial class—for whose democratic views they had almost as much distaste as the Tories—they were at last induced to grant a limited franchise to the middle-class, though this was done only in the belief that it would be of assistance in the traditional contest with the Tory section of the aristocracy.

The workers, who had been the mainstay of the agitation in the country, got nothing for their efforts. The radical reformers had encouraged them to believe that a thorough house-cleaning at Westminster would open the road to their emancipation, but there was never any intention of fulfilling the demagogic promises made to the starving, illiter-ate and desperate masses at the height of the struggle. Angry and disillusioned, and by now experienced in politics, the workers formed their own organizations to take up the fight again.

It was in the Chartist period that followed that socialism became an important political force. But the ground had already been prepared. There were a number of radical writers who influenced the leaders of the growing working-class. Some, like Charles Hall, John Bray, William Thompson, Thomas Hodgskin and John Gray showed a remarkable insight into the character of the new industrial society. They condemned the great maldistribution of wealth and the iniquities of privilege. The mass of the people, they said, was doomed to a life of ignorance, poverty and ill-health. In his brilliant *Lecture on Human Happiness* John Gray developed the idea that exploitation was inherent in the capitalist system, a thesis also advanced by Thompson in his *Distribution of Wealth*, which denounced the capitalist for denying the labourer the reward of his work. Hodgskin, though he was more of an individualist, anticipated the Marxist belief that human history is moulded by economic factors, and argued that the workers would come into their own only after the abolition of class divisions and of government as the instrument by which the rich maintained their rights of property.

The most significant contribution of this group, however, was the use it made of the economics of David Ricardo, the stockbroker, as a foundation of socialist theory. The doctrine that labour is the only source of value and has a right to the whole reward of its efforts was the logical conclusion of Ricardo's argument. It underlay the work of almost every socialist up to and including Marx, who placed it at the centre of his economic analysis.

None of these men, however, can be credited with achievements equal to those of Robert Owen. Born in 1771, apprenticed to a draper at the age of ten, he was the manager of a large mill by the time he was twenty. He was one of the most able industrialists of his time, and soon acquired a considerable fortune. But he was, fortunately, not typical of this class. He held unorthodox views on religion—which were later to be a serious embarrassment to him—and on the importance of environment as a determinant of character. He, practically alone in the early nineteenth century, insisted that decent education, wages and working conditions were essential for the proper development of human personality, and proved by his own example that they were not the road to ruin for manufacturers, as so many believed. In the years of depression after the Napoleonic Wars he began to urge the establishment of co-operative communities along the lines of his remarkable factory at New Lanark. He received some support from the Government to begin with—the Tory Prime Minister, Lord Sidmouth, sent copies of Owen's *New View of Society* to a number of European rulers for their comments—but he was soon attacked both by the ruling class and some of the reformers, one regarding him as a dangerous revolutionary and the other as a reactionary philanthropist.

Owen, in his personal attitude, was certainly a benevolent autocrat, but his teachings soon found a response among the workers. He understood that men could make the most effective use of the vast productive powers of industry if they co-operated for the common good, eliminated private ownership and profit, and set up self-governing industrial and agricultural communities. To prove his point he spent his fortune in a series of futile attempts to establish such colonies in Britain and in the New World. He returned to England in 1829, after spending four years in the United States, to find that the workers had taken up his ideas.

Artisans and factory operatives alike saw in the co-operative community a means by which they could free themselves from the exploitation of the employers, could escape into decent living conditions away from the squalor of the new towns, and, while retaining the valuable features of industry, could regain contact with the land from which they had been driven. A large part of the working-class, after the treachery of the reformers in 1832, was willing to accept a gospel which showed it how direct industrial, rather than political, action could lead it to a democratic and prosperous society.

By 1833 Owen's ideas had a firm hold in the trade unions that were springing up all over the country, and had inspired a number of producer and consumer co-operative enterprises.

John Doherty, one of the outstanding union leaders, was a strong Owenite, and he was associated with Owen in fighting for factory reform and the eight-hour day in the North of England. Owen himself managed to establish the Grand National Consolidated Trades Union, which, at its height, claimed over half a million members.

The unions which composed this body did not confine themselves to agitation on wages and hours. They attempted to set up workshops which would compete with those of their masters and eventually drive them out of business. Rejecting political action in the electoral sense, for a time they favoured the idea of a general strike as a means of transition to the new society of co-operation and equality. But, for all its hopes, the movement crumbled as fast as it was built, its strength wasted in a series of exhausting strikes and lock-outs.

The savage sentence passed upon the Tolpuddle land-workers in 1834 for their attempt to form a branch of Owen's union was answered by protest meetings throughout Britain, but the prosecution accelerated the disintegration of the Grand National Consolidated Trades Union. In little less than a year after its foundation it was wound up and the active leadership of the working-class passed from Owen into other hands.

Owen himself lived on for another twenty years, but his work was done. He had produced a coherent socialist philosophy—even the word "socialism" was first used in an Owenite paper—and built a great though short-lived movement. Finally, it was his ideas that inspired the Rochdale Equitable Pioneers to start the modern movement of consumers' co-operation in 1844.

Almost immediately after the collapse of the Owenite movement, and while Owen's doctrine still found widespread support, the British working-class again took up the struggle for the political rights which they had failed to win in the agitation for the Reform Act. For the next ten years, while the men of property trembled at the prospect of revolution, the demand for the People's Charter was pressed forward by vast demonstrations, petitions, riots, and even sporadic attempts at rebellion. Chartism—and this was one of the reasons for its ultimate failure—was not a homogeneous movement. To some of its supporters the platform of universal suffrage, annual parliaments and payment for members was sufficient for an immediate end. Others, however, regarded it as merely the first step along the road to a socialist republic. Both revolutionaries and reformists agreed that political power should be secured by the working-class. But there was no common opinion about the way that power should be won or about the use that should be made of it after victory.

William Lovett and his associates in the London Working Men's Association, who first drew up the Charter in 1837, were skilled artisans who believed in patient and rational propaganda for reform. They had no intention of leading a mass movement which often threatened to turn into a national insurrection, and were quite prepared to work with the radical elements of the middle-class within and without Parliament to carry the Charter.

But events moved too rapidly for them. Following the passage of the Poor Law Amendment Act in 1834, at a time when the conditions of life for the factory operatives and land-workers were literally murderous, the old system of subsidizing wages from the rates was abolished, and the poor driven into workhouses, where deliberate starvation and cruelty were the rule. The Poor Law agitation in the industrial North could not be halted by repression. It quickly came under the leadership of the Chartists, who were the only group capable of giving it coherence and organization. The struggle for the Charter, by peaceful or violent means, seemed the only hope for men ground down by the joint despotism of capitalism and the ruling oligarchy.

Chartism failed, though it at one time had a majority behind it. There was no chance of arresting capitalist develop-ment in Britain at that stage or of an immature working-class movement winning its battle with the new alliance of landlords and industrialists. Nevertheless, the Chartist movement was the first mass proletarian organization to attempt this task. It was a school in which socialist theory and tactics were taught, not only to the British workers but to the European workers as well.

Though it declined rapidly at the end of the 'forties,

it had a lasting influence in the nineteenth century. It was divided, as all socialist movements have since been split, between reformists with a devotion to constitutional procedure and a revolutionary wing which believed that the working-class could only triumph by a violent assault upon a State which they saw as an instrument of capitalist domination. The two groups fought for the leadership of the movement, and each blamed its failure on the follies of the other. Neither, at that time, could have secured the desired success. In its absence the British workers turned to other methods, to support the cheap bread agitation of the Anti-Corn Law League, to consumers' co-operation, to the construction of non-socialist trade unionism and, on the whole, a policy of sharing to a small extent in the wealth which capitalism was bringing to Britain from every corner of the world.

Yet this short survey of Chartism would not be complete without some mention of men such as George Julian Harney and Bronterre O'Brien. Both of them were extreme socialists and both were strongly influenced by the French Revolution.

In articles—chiefly in the *Poor Man's Guardian* and the Chartist *Northern Star*—in pamphlets and speeches, Harney and O'Brien continually took a wider view of the struggle than most of their contemporaries, and attempted to thrash out a working-class philosophy which would both explain and justify what they were trying to do. O'Brien translated Buonarotti's history of Babeuf's communist conspiracy. Though, later in life, he became lost in a confusion of his own economic ideas, in the Chartist period he was far ahead of most of his fellow propagandists in his perception that working-class misery was due to the structure of capitalist industry rather than to the personal villainy of the employers. He had a clear understanding of the nature and importance of the class struggle.

Unlike many of the Chartists, including their most prominent leader, the fiery demagogue Feargus O'Connor, he did not wish to substitute peasant smallholdings for the tyranny of the machine, but realized that industry could be made the servant instead of the master of the worker. He attacked both Church and State as means by which property held the people in subjection. He fought the idea of Owen and the other utopian socialists that society could be converted by example and that the capture of political power was unimportant. In short, he had moved a long way towards the theories that Marx and Engels were to weave together in the doctrine of historical materialism. Harney, unlike O'Brien, was a young man at the peak of the Chartist movement: though he was one of the most powerful supporters of revolutionary methods for carrying the Charter, he never rivalled the theoretical brilliance of O'Brien, and his importance is due more to the way he maintained the socialist tradition after Chartism disintegrated—in spite of his instability and his political egotism—than to his merits as a thinker. In many respects Marxism stands in the direct line of descent from Chartism. Together with Ernest Jones, another of the younger Chartists, Harney represents the link between the two.

Chartism was not socialism, but it provided the experience upon which socialism and the working-class movement could be built. Before the further development of industry raised new problems and also fresh possibilities for the workers, they had experimented with constitutionalism, with the general strike, and with insurrection, all three methods upon which modern movements have relied. They had come to realize that the wheels of progress could not be reversed and the lost glories of peasant farming restored. Capitalism, it was clear, had come to stay, and they had to make terms with it. Though the revolutionary tradition never died out, the mass of the British working-class was ready to improve its conditions of life within the existing system. It was not willing to waste its strength in futile efforts to overthrow it. After the fiasco of the last major Chartist demonstration in April 1848, at a time when the European proletariat was on the barricades, the marriage between socialism and the working-class movement was temporarily dissolved in Britain. The elaboration of socialist doctrine went on steadily, but it had comparatively little influence on the men who were building up their new trade union and co-operative organizations.

CHAPTER IV

FRANCE AND GERMANY

THE Powers which defeated Napoleonic France met in the Congress of Vienna in 1815. They tried to make a settlement which would not only lessen the danger of recurrent war, but also check the social unrest and agitation that was spreading throughout Europe. In the first task they were successful for four decades; in the second they were defeated by the alliance of liberalism and nationalism, and by the fact that the growth of capitalist industry released new political and economic forces which steadily undermined the European structure built and maintained by Metternich as a bulwark against reform.

The working-class developed later and more spasmodically in Europe than in Britain. In the years before 1848 it was only important in a few centres—Paris, for instance—where it worked politically as the Left wing of the democratic and republican movement. In some countries the awakening of national consciousness distracted attention from social issues and united the people against foreign despotism. Until the national question was settled in lands like Italy, Poland and, to a lesser extent, Germany, there was little chance of any significant socialist thought or organization making much headway. The peasantry, up to at least the middle of the nineteenth century, was the predominant group in all European States, and on the whole it was deeply religious, hostile to the towns, and a prop for any strong government.

The history of these years is the struggle between the ideas launched on the world by the French Revolution and the old autocratic and backward monarchies which still sought to arrest the development of liberty, democracy and industry. In almost every country of Europe this issue was fought out. In some the revolutionaries sought to liberate their nation; in others the liberals demanded a constitution. Everywhere the conservatives found themselves on the defensive. Their police were continually unearthing conspiracies organized by the secret societies in which the revolutionaries were forced by persecution to organize. There certainly was not any central organization directing the activities of the liberals in every nation, but, in the words of the chief of the Paris police in 1825, "they had one language, one code of morality, one religion, a common political aim". It was in these conditions that socialism emerged in France and Germany.

In July 1830 Charles X was overthrown by a revolution in Paris. The Bourbon monarchy, reimposed on France by the victorious Powers in 1815, which represented the wealthy landowners and such of the old aristocracy as had survived the guillotine, was replaced by a new régime. Charles was succeeded by Louis Philippe, Duke of Orleans, who was sponsored by the financiers and speculators who had enriched themselves at the expense of the State and the peasantry.

It was not long before the radicals and republicans realized that they had manned the barricades only to bring the bankers to power. The secret societies again became active. There was an abortive insurrection in 1832 in Paris, and another at Lyons in 1834. In 1839 conspirators belonging to the Society of the Seasons seized the Paris Town Hall before their revolt was crushed. The leader of the society was Auguste Blanqui, an extraordinary man who spent a great deal of his life serving a series of prison sentences and the remainder in organizing the revolutionary workpeople of Paris.

Blanqui was essentially a pupil of Gracchus Babeuf.

He had learnt at first-hand the ideas and methods of the Conspiracy of the Equals from Philippe Buonarroti, its historian, with whom he had been associated in the Parisian secret societies, and tried to apply them with little modification to the France of his time. Blanqui, however, was more realistic than most of his contemporary socialists in France and Germany. He, unlike the utopians, based his revolutionary tactics upon the class struggle of the workers against the capitalists and landlords who exploited and dictated to them. He was not much concerned with working out a detailed analysis of society or of the proletarian republic he wished to establish. On the other hand, he underestimated both the importance of the liberal effort to secure political democracy and of mass working-class organization. Blanqui placed his faith in a *putsch* accomplished by a small disciplined group of professional conspirators as a surprise assault, without any preliminary attempt to educate or prepare a large number of workers to support it.

Throughout his life—and he lived to see the Paris Commune of 1871—Blanqui never shook off the traditional methods of the secret society. As a result, in spite of his personal heroism and the services he rendered to French socialism in the days when both it and he were young, he could not understand or participate in the new movements which grew up after the revolutionary upheavals of 1848. He, and those whom he inspired and led, remained an influential group in French socialism until after the suppression of the Paris Commune. But their energy and devotion to the cause were never matched by their achievements: they were frequently a source of friction and embarrassment in the wider socialist movement.

Neither Blanqui's ideas nor his methods could provide an adequate philosophy for the majority of the French workers. For this they turned elsewhere, above all to Louis Blanc and to Pierre-Joseph Proudhon. These two men differed widely in personality and outlook, but between them they provided most of the intellectual inspiration of the mass socialist movement.

Louis Blanc was the first socialist of any importance to believe that the State could be used as an instrument of reform rather than as a machine for the domination of one class by another. He could not accept Blanqui's argument that liberal reforms were mere hypocrisy and that the working-class could achieve its salvation only by an insurrection which would be followed by a dictatorship directed against the rich. He supported the agitation for universal suffrage on the grounds that a democratically elected government could first alleviate the misery of the people and then, gradually, replace competitive capitalism by co-operative factories and services. In 1839, at the age of twenty-eight, he published his best book, *The Organisation of Work*. In it he suggested that the State should set up social workshops, supplying capital and machinery for the purpose. The mines, banks and railways, taken over by the State, would provide its revenue. The workers would learn the art of management; their right to employment would be guaranteed; and the capitalists he so brilliantly indicted would be given the option of joining the system of workshops or being driven out of business by their superior efficiency.

Blanc, to use a modern phrase, was a reformist. He was more concerned with working out practical schemes upon which France could immediately be set to work than with agitating the Paris masses to revolt in the name of millenial socialist doctrines. His insistence upon the right to work and his plan for national workshops, it is true, stirred many of those who fought in the 1848 insurrections, but he was in many ways the forerunner of later gradualist socialism, with its belief that, in time, it would attain power by electoral methods and proceed, by steady if slow steps, to use the existing State as a means of securing both economic stability and the better welfare of its working-class.

During 1848, when Blanc himself was a junior member of the revolutionary government, national workshops were actually set up to absorb some of the unemployed. Though they retained the name which Blanc had popularized, they were intended by his non-socialist colleagues in the Provisional Government to be a failure. They were tried only to damp down working-class agitation and to discredit Blanc himself by their futility. From 1852 until 1870 Blanc was an exile in London. He returned to France and, in spite of his claim that he was still a socialist, opposed the proletarian and revolutionary Paris Commune.

Proudhon was a very different type of man. He was neither successful nor realistic. His thought suffered from a lack of intellectual discipline. He was capable of brilliant criticism of other doctrines and parties, but he was unable to bind his own ideas with consistency or to purge them of serious confusions. He was self-educated and, though he had read very widely, never properly digested his material. In spite of his lasting influence on French socialism he never understood the character of the urban working-class, and until his death his outlook was dominated by the peasant background from which he sprang and the artisans among whom he lived. Nevertheless, he made a great impression in his day, and as recently as 1919 there was a Proudhonist revival in France as a reaction against the growing strength of Marxism.

Proudhon was essentially an individualist. He attacked the existing property relationships on the grounds that they frustrated the adequate development of human personality, which he believed was sacred above all else. The peasant is the individual at his best, for in an agricultural society a man fulfils himself in living by his own personal and direct efforts. Many of the earlier socialists, especially the primitives and utopians, had denounced the family as an obstacle to progress, but for Proudhon it is the only really good form of social organization. Through the family, man learns to appreciate the moral virtues of justice, liberty, equality and chastity, the last of which is the greatest, for without it the family cannot survive. The possession of property is evil if it enables the owner to live without work, good if he uses it as a means to work. (In other words, landlords are as undesirable as peasant ownership is laudable.)

Proudhon not only disliked a State dominated by bankers; he condemned all States on principle. "Government of man by man in every form is oppression," he wrote, for "the highest perfection of society is found in the union of order and anarchy". Since the function of any State must be to protect property and privilege, it must be replaced by a federation of self-governing communes in which there would be neither rich nor poor, master nor servant.

Thus Proudhon's emphasis on the individual made him the protagonist of anarchism, of a society so free from the twin tyrannies of wealth and power that there would be no restrictions upon the liberty of the individual to fulfil himself as best he might. Proudhon's economic views were, if anything, as popular as his politics. In 1846 he published his *System of Economic Contradictions*, in which he argued that the social character of a society is determined more by the manner in which wealth circulates than by the methods by which it is produced. Therefore changes should be accomplished by alterations in the credit system. To this end he called for the establishment of credit banks which would lend money without interest and act as the centre of producers' co-operation. This idea swept through the workers in Paris and a few other towns.

At that time trade unions were prohibited in France, and in addition, owing to the late development of French industry, most workers were employed in small workshops. Thrown back upon themselves, the workers naturally took up a doctrine which placed individualism above collective organization, and seemed to offer them the chance of becoming masters in their own right. Proudhon was certainly not a socialist in the normal sense. In many ways his views are reactionary, for he was trying to stop the development of both the State and a modern economic system he could not properly analyse. Though he had a far greater status than his doctrine justifies, his protest against the conditions in which the French working-class knew itself to be living and his imprisonment for making that protest made him a teacher and a martyr.

Up to the revolt of February 1848 the Paris workers were by no means a distinct and organized opposition to the régime of Louis Philippe, though large numbers of them were active supporters of one of the socialist groups—of Louis Blanc, of Proudhon, of Blanqui, of the utopian communist Cabet, who wished to found an idyllic colony in the New World, of even the Saint-Simonians and the Fourierists.

The 1848 Revolution was a united effort by the middle-class and the workers to remove the corrupt monarchy, the government which Karl Marx later described as "nothing other than a joint stock company for the exploitation of French national wealth". The middle-class, which wanted to curb the financiers and speculators, and to stabilize expenditure which threatened to ruin the developing industry and commerce of France, split in two groups after the revolt succeeded. The first, representing the industrialists, desired a constitutional monarchy and some extension of the franchise; the second, based on the small merchants and business men, was more radical and favoured a republic.

After three months of uneasy compromise the Right wing

won and succeeded in provoking the workers into an abortive insurrection, which was ruthlessly crushed. In the June fighting the Paris workers emerged as an independent political force for the first time, while the radical section of the middle-class deserted the Jacobin tradition and sided with the counter-revolution. The workers did not revolt in the name of socialism, but in their desperate misery they turned for leadership to socialists of many kinds, who offered some chance of an improvement in their lot. Up to this turning-point in European history the working-class had not been clearly distinguished from the mass of "citizens" with radical views. After June 1848 the road lay open for new kinds of socialist theory and organization based unambiguously upon the proletariat and directed against the capitalists who had at last become the masters of France.

Events in Germany followed a different course. The country was divided into a multitude of petty principalities. Though Prussia dominated them increasingly until it finally accomplished the unification of the German States into a nation, this task took nearly three-quarters of the nineteenth century. In Germany the struggle for national unity went hand in hand with the liberal demand for constitutional rights, bitterly opposed by both the rulers and their attendant bureaucracies in the greater and lesser States.

The Rhineland, however, was more advanced than the rest of the country owing to its more developed commerce and industry, and owing to its occupation by the French, and was the strongest centre of the reform movement. After 1813, in the revolutionary war against Napoleon, some progress was made, though neither the land reform nor the grant of limited political rights to the people was particularly far-reaching or effective. In spite of sporadic activity, German liberalism was a weak and immature force. Owing to the social conditions in the country, it was born late and suffered from a feeling of timidity and inferiority. It never engaged in a head-on clash with the old society as had its counterparts in England and France. Disunited, backward, reactionary, Germany was not a fertile soil for revolutionary organization. The most intelligent and far-seeing thinkers were

compelled to confine themselves largely to intellectual speculation, for want of opportunity to do anything else, as the poet
Heine so brilliantly said in this satirical epigram:

> The French and Russians rule the land,
> The English rule the sea;
> But we in the airy realm of dreams
> Hold sovereign mastery.

This Germany produced great philosophers, of whom two at
least—Fichte and Hegel—are the masters of much in later
socialist thought. Of these Hegel was by far the more important.

The Hegelian philosophy could be interpreted in two ways.
On one side it was an extremely sophisticated defence of things
as they were; on the other, in the hands of a group known as the
Young Hegelians, it developed into a number of different
socialist schools of which the most outstanding was Marxism.
Hegel as a conservative passed out of history with his times;
Hegel as a man who revolutionized European philosophy
remains an active influence today. He established the doctrine
that change occurs in any field only as a result of a struggle
between conflicting forces; that truth was not a collection of
dogmatic statements which men could painfully assemble and
then learn by rote; and that neither history nor knowledge can
stand still at a pinnacle of achievement. History, said Hegel,
is a continuous process. Each and every society is but a land-
mark on the endless pilgrimage of humanity from lower to
higher states of life. This evolutionary process conforms to
definite laws of development which can be ascertained and
which, once discovered, can be used to chart the general
direction in which a society is moving.

These ideas had tremendous possibilities as a means of
analysis, and the Young Hegelians quickly seized the opportunity thus offered. They made penetrating criticisms of
politics, history, religion, morals and even aesthetics. But, for
all their brilliance, none of them rivalled a young doctor of
philosophy called Karl Marx, who, denied a lectureship at the
University of Bonn by the reactionary authorities, had turned
to liberal journalism.

Marx was born in Trèves in 1818, of a Jewish family which had been converted to Christianity. By the time he was twenty-six his experiences as editor of the liberal *Rheinische Zeitung* had already led him to make a thorough study of the work of French socialist writers. When, for his activity, he was forced to emigrate to Paris, he had already worked out the basis of the materialist socialist philosophy which has ever since borne his name. In Paris, in 1844, he came to know Heine, Proudhon and a host of other radical and proletarian revolutionaries, among them the man who was to be his lifelong friend and colleague, Friedrich Engels, the son of a prosperous Rhineland manufacturer and, like Marx, a Young Hegelian. In a symposium published by Marx in 1844 he included an article by Engels which, taken together with the latter's book on the working-class in England—written at the age of twenty-four after he had made a study of the Chartist Movement and come to know many prominent Chartists—shows that Engels had travelled a road similar to Marx in developing Hegel's dialectical philosophy into a socialist analysis of capitalist society.

From that moment on they collaborated as thinkers and organizers alike. When Marx was forced to leave Paris through the intervention of the Prussian Government, he went to Brussels and, joined at times by Engels, remained there until the outbreak of the revolutions of 1848, studying economics and political thought. In this period he and Engels produced *The Holy Family*, a polemic against their fellow Young Hegelians, and *The German Ideology*, a similar work; Marx alone wrote *The Poverty of Philosophy*, an attack on Proudhon's doctrine.

These books are important, for they reveal the way in which Marx developed his own ideas and, at the same time, they contain a much more explicit statement of some parts of his philosophy than he was ever to write again. For, by 1848, Marx had done the groundwork on which historical material-ism rests. Later, he extended this to an analysis of the economic structure of society, embodied in his great work, *Capital*, and to practical problems of politics. Neither Marx nor Engels believed that it was possible to codify their views into a fixed and final system of thought. They continually insisted that they had worked out a *method* of analysing and tackling social and historical questions, not a philosophy which anyone could learn from a textbook. Their lives, as much as their books, are the sources to which the student of Marxism must turn. All the time they were actively organizing the international working-class movement they were refining, extending and applying their basic theories to the changing state of European society. Marxism, true to its Hegelian parentage, has never stood still. That makes it particularly difficult to do more than summarize its most essential principles in a book such as this.

CHAPTER V

MARXIST PHILOSOPHY

THE revolutions of 1848 were a turning-point in European history. From Spain to Poland the Continent was torn by civil war as liberals and nationalists struggled for democracy and independence. The working-class, still a minority, played only a subordinate role, acting, as in England, as the radical wing of the liberal revolt. After 1848, as industry developed across the Continent, independent working-class organizations also spread, this time as the opponents instead of the allies of the middle-class of commerce and industry. The new master was the capitalist, and to many workers he seemed worse than those overthrown by the democratic insurrections. Eighteen-forty-eight, in fact, was the year in which the modern socialist movement, based on the class struggle against industrial capitalism, really begins. In Europe, at least, that development was given direction and coherence by Marxism.

Both Marx and Engels played a part in the revolution in Germany, but, when the movement failed, went into exile for the rest of their lives. German liberalism was too weak to succeed. Its leaders, moreover, were so terrified that their victory might open the way for the socialists that they preferred to make a compromise with the Junkers and bureaucrats rather than press their revolt too far. We have already seen how, in France, the Right had chosen to shoot down the Paris workers in thousands rather than share the fruits of the struggle with them. This action taught the moderate reformers in Germany a sharp lesson. Elsewhere in Europe the revolutionaries were too preoccupied with winning national freedom to bother much with social questions. Where they did, land reform seemed more important to them than the agitation of a handful of socialists in countries where the peasantry predominated, and there was no working-class in any real sense.

In none of the struggles of 1848 did the initiative lie with the working-class. Nevertheless, apart from the political experience gained by the workers, there was one development which completely transformed the character of socialism.

Marx and Engels, in emigration, had been brought into close contact with the secret societies and clubs formed by socialists and communists—many of them refugees from Germany—in Paris, Brussels, London and a few other towns. Among these groups was one called the League of the Just. During 1846 and 1847 Marx and Engels had won over the majority of the League to their way of thinking, and it was reorganized as the Communist League. At the end of 1847 they were instructed to draw up a programme for this body. In a few weeks the work was done, and the *Communist Manifesto* was published early in 1848.

It has been the most influential single document in the history of socialism, circulating up to our own time in millions of copies and translated into almost every language. For the first time it provided a basis upon which the socialist movement could be built as an organized and coherent party, as distinct from the sects and conspiracies into which it was divided up to and during 1848. It set the day-to-day experiences of the working-class against the background of history and gave them a meaning. It showed that proletarian misery was the result of a social system, not of the tyranny and evil of particular men; that this system could be changed only after a period of hard organization and propaganda, culminating in the overthrow of capitalism by force; that reckless conspiracy was as futile as the utopian belief that capitalists could be persuaded to change their ways either by reason or example; and that the only hope of emancipating the workers from economic slavery was the activity of the workers themselves. Above all—and this is undoubtedly the secret of its influence—it was aimed less at providing an answer to immediate problems than at setting out a philosophy which would be a valid guide to the working-class up to and even after the day when it finally seized power. Marx and Engels certainly developed and revised some of the ideas which are put forward in the *Communist Manifesto*, especially on the side of analysis, but its scope is so wide and its picture of social development is so penetrating that it has been retained as a classic theoretical text for the socialist movement up to the present.

What did Marx and Engels say in the *Manifesto* and in their later writings which, for convenience, may be taken with it at this point?

History, they said, was not a succession of accidental events but a continuous process of social development according to a definite pattern. This conception they took from Hegel. With it they adopted Hegel's dialectical philosophy which stated that all change is the result of conflicts between diametrically opposed forces, which, in negating each other, produce a new and higher synthesis. For Hegel this took place primarily on the plane of ideas. Marx, on the other hand, applied this principle to human society. In a famous phrase of the *Manifesto* he declared that history consisted of class struggles. Every society is based upon a definite system of production. The character of that system, the way in which wealth is produced —by slaves, serfs, peasants or factory workers—determines the social and political pattern of that society. In every society, moreover, there is a ruling class which owns the means of production.

But new productive techniques develop, offering the prospect of increased wealth and command over nature. With them develop new classes which demand changes in social and economic organization, at the expense of the old class of rulers. One mode of production becomes obsolete and a fetter upon the development of society. The class associated with the new methods endeavours to break down the restrictions upon their proper employment, and it is thus brought into direct and revolutionary conflict with the property relationships and with the State power of the old ruling class. This, for Marxism, is the law of social evolution.

In Western civilization, Marx said, slavery had given place to feudalism, since the latter used the material and labour resources of society more efficiently. At the close of the Middle Ages feudalism itself had become a brake on economic progress. The merchant class, the bourgeoisie, fought the feudal aristocracy to break down the restrictions upon the use and expansion of wealth, to substitute wage-labour for serfdom, free enterprise for the stagnant medieval economy which was unable to take advantage of the opportunities offered by an expanding commerce, and by the discovery of the New World. Since it was based on a dynamic and developing system of production, the bourgeoisie was bound to triumph in the long revolutionary struggle—of which both the English Civil War and the French Revolution were a part—to clear away the remnants of feudal life from ground on which industrial capitalism was later built.

But as the economic foundations of society changed, so also did the property relationships, the political ideas and institutions, even the religion and the culture. Thus the whole range of man's social activities was raised to a higher and more complex level. This, however, did not mean that capitalist society was either stable or enduring, though Marx continually insisted that it was the most advanced form of social organization that was possible for a long period in history. There would come a point, he argued, at which capitalism would, in its turn, be obsolete and bar the progress of humanity towards a richer and more prosperous society. Technical and economic development, Marx saw, would open new perspectives to man, would awaken hopes which capitalism would be unable to satisfy without destroying the very methods of production and exchange on which it rested. Unable to advance any further, having completed its mission, having knit the world into an interdependent economic system, capitalism would break up in a series of wars and revolutions. Once again a new class would rise to power, establishing a different system of production, novel forms of government, a fresh set of values and ethics. Just as the bourgeoisie developed the democratic ideology in its revolutionary youth, so this new class, the proletariat, would have its own philosophy, socialism. Marx believed, however, that the destiny of the working-class was to introduce a new kind of society in which, after some time, there would be neither opposing classes nor poverty.

Why did Marx state with such conviction that capitalism would disintegrate and that the proletariat would desire and be able to conquer power?

In the first place Marx realized that there was much more

pitalist system than many of his contemporaries
d. For them it was certainly an immoral and inequit-
able method of controlling the productive resources of a
country. But they could not grasp the significance of the
changes that were taking place within the structure of capitalism as the nineteenth century wore on. The inherent tendency
of capitalist industrial enterprise, said Marx, is towards
monopolistic control, towards larger and more efficient plants,
thus eliminating unnecessary competition between the producers. As capitalism extends its scope, this process is repeated
on an international scale. Inside a country individual firms
compete for a market, seeking the maximum profit for themselves and the bankruptcy of their rivals. In the same way,
capitalist nations strive to gain control of as much of the world
as they can, both as a source of raw material and as a market
for their products. This imperialist drive leads inevitably to
war, since each capitalist State must try to be more powerful
than its competitors. Capital cannot lie idle: it must expand or
perish.

Secondly, capitalism changes the character of labour. It is a
condition of industrial production that it must draw together
large numbers of workers under the same roof, in the same firm,
in the same industry. The worker is no longer an individual:
he is a unit in a process which is based upon collective effort.
His personal fate is no longer dependent upon his ability to
wrest a living from a plot of land or to turn out goods by hand
in a small workshop. He is increasingly divorced from either
ownership or direction of the means of production on which
he relies to earn his keep; his condition of life is determined
by events beyond his control; by, for instance, price fluctuations on some distant exchange or by the development of new
techniques.

Yet the further this process goes, the more it unites the
workers into a coherent and self-conscious class. In a particular
factory they combine against a single employer; in an industry,
against a group of them. From this it is but a logical step to
unite against capitalists as a class and private enterprise as a
system. Moreover, modern capitalism, at the same time as it
increases the rivalry between nations, makes them more

dependent upon each other. Since capitalism is an international system, it is natural and necessary that the workers, who have similar experiences and aspirations in all countries, should also organize internationally. Production, Marx understood, had changed from a handicraft to a social function. He saw that the more powerful private ownership became, the more it socialized the processes of production, drawing into an integrated whole ever-wider circles of the population. Therefore, he argued, a stage will be reached where the social character of industrial activity will conflict with its direction by one class of the community. Society is then ripe for radical change. Its social and political relationships must be reorganized to correspond with the socialization of its economy. This is something that cannot be done until power has been wrested from the bourgeoisie and ownership of the land and factories transferred to the State. Marx, however, always insisted that the workers could not seize power until this point of crisis was reached. As long as capitalism was an expanding system, not having exhausted the possibilities of development within itself, it would survive. As soon as it began to contract it was a sign that its day was over and that it would have to make way for a new system.

The brilliant prophecy that capitalism would, indeed, enter a period of decline, made at a period when it seemed all-powerful, was the third reason that Marx advanced for his belief in the ultimate victory of the working-class, though he undoubtedly expected this victory at a comparatively early date, in his lifetime. It was based upon a lifetime's study of the inner structure of capitalist enterprise. The basis of Marxian economics was not new.

We have already seen how a group of early English socialists had taken Ricardo's argument a stage further and developed the theory that labour was the sole source of value. Marx placed this concept at the centre of his analysis. The worker, he said, by his labour, creates the value of a product. But he does not receive in wages the full equivalent. The difference between what he is paid and what the product may eventually fetch for his master, after other production costs have been met, is what Marx termed "surplus-value",

D

the source of the rents, interest and profits upon which the class of capitalists exists.

Since there is a gap between the total value of production and the purchasing power distributed in wages and salaries—and this gap is extended by the sharp gradations in the income-structure of capitalist society, and by the character of investment methods—capitalism, over a period, is unable to sell all the goods it produces. The more that the share of labour is reduced, or, at least, frozen in relation to the expansion of production, in the search for lower costs and higher profits, the greater the difficulty that capitalism encounters in finding markets. For a time this problem can be solved by selling manufactures to less-developed peoples. But, as capitalism brings more nations within its scope, industrialism appears in these countries and they become competitors. The capitalists of the more advanced States, by the export of capital, themselves promote this rivalry. The rate of profit all capitalists secure thus tends to fall on average. They are, therefore, driven, on the one hand, to reduce costs by improving technique or by lowering wages, or both, and on the other to try and exclude their rivals from definite markets, spheres of influence and colonial territories.

These processes lead to increasing inability to postpone a crisis within any capitalist system and, between competing systems, to imperialist struggles. By the time the world is divided between a few powerful imperialist States, the general crisis of capitalism will begin. Internally, it will be unable to overcome the gulf between production and purchasing power; abroad, the attempt to secure markets can only lead to world wars unequalled in their scope and cost. The epoch of the proletarian revolution has arrived.

Marx, however, was not a fatalist. He did not believe that the downfall of capitalism would lead inevitably to the victory of the working-class. Men, he insists continually, make their own history, and within certain limits set for them by the conditions of their time have a considerable amount of free choice. Therefore it is necessary to work actively for the socialist cause, not to wait until the millenium arrives of its own accord. Though the working-class may be brought into conflict with capitalism as a result of its social experience, the consequent protest must be organized into a coherent force. There can be a class-struggle which never results in the triumph of the proletariat because it has not been canalized into organization by leaders who understand the laws of social change. It is this that is the task of revolutionary socialists. By relating day-to-day developments to the whole historical movement for working-class emancipation, they can make the working-class conscious of itself as a class and of its role as the one group in society capable of leading humanity forward.

Trade unions, Marx argued, are the primary organizations of the workers, and arise spontaneously. Their activities are largely confined to economic and industrial matters, such as the level of wages or the regulation of working conditions. But, Marx said, the capitalist class against which trade unions organize controls the State and dominates the intellectual and cultural life of society. Therefore the workers must form a political party to match the efforts of the trade unions. This party would carry the class-struggle into every sphere, municipal and national politics, philosophy, literature, the courts, the armed forces and even religion. It would not be sufficient for it to catch the votes of the workers year by year until it secured a parliamentary majority—though Marx conceded that this might be possible in some exceptional cases—since if the bourgeoisie faced a mounting political and economic crisis it would be quite capable of suppressing both the workers' party and its own democratic institutions. The working-class movement must be prepared to overthrow the bourgeoisie by force, for it would never voluntarily yield the State power it fought so hard to secure and maintain.

Once this has been done the workers must set up their own State—Marx uses the famous phrase here: a dictatorship of the proletariat which will effectively prevent a counter-revolution and pave the way for the classless society in which there will no longer be any need for the State as an instrument of class rule. Men, for the first time in history, will then be really free. Society can enjoy peace, since neither class antagonism nor war will disrupt it. There will be a rapid increase in social welfare because industry and agriculture will be operated for service and not for profit. The only limits on production will be the scarcity of the earth's resources and the degree to which man is able to harness them to his own ends. Both Marx and Engels were convinced that limitless opportunities of advance lay before mankind once its energy was no more squandered in social struggles and was devoted to the proper and extended use of its great technical discoveries. For them the victory of socialism marked the day on which the childhood of the human race would end and, conscious of the laws of science and society, men would begin to work together in a creative unity for their common prosperity and fulfilment.

This remarkable philosophy, of which only a bare outline has been given here, has been the most important single contribution to socialist theory. If much of it is accepted as commonplace today, that is a measure of the way Marxism has influenced the views we hold about the development and pattern of contemporary society, just as Darwinism revolutionized our concept of nature. Since Marx died his ideas have been refined and carried further, notably by Lenin. But no other socialist has ever done such a monumental service to his cause.

CHAPTER VI

THE YEARS OF FRUSTRATION

THE years after 1848 were a difficult time for European socialism. The working-class groups had failed to take the initiative from the middle-class parties or to make any serious impression on the course of events during the revolutionary upheaval. Many of the leaders were driven into exile. Those who remained behind were either in prison or escaping the attentions of the police, and they had little opportunity to rally their disorganized and disillusioned supporters. In England, the Chartist demonstration of April 1848, which the Government had feared might be the signal for a revolt, ended in a fiasco which finished Chartism as a mass movement. The socialists in emigration spent their strength in hatching wild schemes for fresh insurrections, in recrimination about their failures, and in doctrinal controversy. It took the movement twenty years to recover from the setbacks of 1848. Throughout those years, it is true, there was an undercurrent of activity, but until the lessons of 1848 had been assimilated no headway could be made. The changed political and economic conditions in Europe required different methods from those which the old ideas and leaders could offer. Until they were pushed to one side, and until the further development of industry had produced another and more class-conscious generation of workers, the movement was doomed to be politically ineffective. Socialism, in fact, had to make a fresh start. It was only in the early 'sixties that this became possible.

Although the agitation of Ferdinand Lassalle in Germany after 1862, and the foundation of the International Working-men's Association in 1864—the body now called the First International—were the first real signs of a revival, some important work was done by the men who kept socialism alive in the years of stagnation. Most of them were in London, where political refugees from almost every European country had gathered. Together with a small group of Chartists who had belonged to the revolutionary wing of the movement, they tried to keep an organizational nucleus going against the day when mass activity would once more be practicable. Of course, this work was hindered and diverted by factional disputes.

But for all their weaknesses, the socialists in London did their best to carry on. For a while both Marx and Engels refused to play any part in *émigré* politics, for they were disgusted with its petty squabbles and futile intrigues. But, as the memory of 1848 faded and some of the more tiresome people dropped out or emigrated to America, they both worked actively with the revolutionaries in London, and gradually, as the influence of Marxism grew, became the two outstanding figures in international socialism. Their life in emigration was not easy. Engels, it is true, rose to be a most successful business man, but he had to support the Marx family most of the time. He did this willingly so that Marx would be free to devote his energies to study and political work. He modestly regarded this as one of the ways in which he could best contribute to the development of the philosophy and the movement to which they both gave their lives.

Engels, however, was not the passive colleague of Marx. He took a full share in their joint theoretical work, and after Marx died he not only went on with his own writing, but he also edited two further volumes of *Capital* from the notes that Marx had left. The partnership of these two men, in thought and in action, was remarkable. There have been few friendships so intimate or fruitful.

Both Marx and Engels were organizers as well as thinkers. Their literary studies were pursued not as ends in themselves, but as practical assets for the political struggle. Early in his career Marx used a phrase that might have served as a motto for them both. "The philosophers have only *interpreted* the world in different ways," he wrote; "the point, however, is to *change* it." By 1848 Marx knew what his interpretation was. With some success he set about changing the world.

The work of the First International was the greatest practical achievement of Marx himself. But while he was the moving spirit behind it, he was not its founder. From some accounts, indeed, it would appear that it was created almost by accident. On the contrary, the International was preceded by a number of attempts to form an international working-class organization, without which its own efforts could not have met with such success.

The English workers had shown sympathy towards revolutionary movements on the Continent as early as the agitation for the Reform Bill. Later, Chartist newspapers such as the *Northern Star* had encouraged the idea of international solidarity and had given a good deal of their space to reports of developments abroad, while foreign refugees took part in many Chartist demonstrations. In 1845 the Society of Fraternal Democrats was set up to act as a clearing-house for international information. It included representatives from almost all the countries in Europe. George Julian Harney was among its foremost members. It was not a separate party but a propagandist body, based on a communist platform which denounced national prejudices and declared that all men were brothers and equals.

By 1847 the Fraternal Democrats were well known outside England, and many of the foreign democratic papers reprinted their manifestos. In the last months of 1847 Marx arrived in London from Brussels to discuss with them the possibility of holding an international workers' congress. Harney had suggested this idea. It was frustrated, however, by the confusion of events in 1848. But, more than eighteen months before the slogan "Workers of all lands, unite!" was given immortality in the *Communist Manifesto*, Harney was saying the same thing to the socialists in London. Harney and Ernest Jones, one of the younger Chartist leaders who also became a communist, were members of a delegation which visited Paris in March 1848 to greet the French revolutionaries.

After 1848 the Fraternal Democrats declined in strength and influence. With the collapse of the proletarian groups on the Continent and the drift of the English workers away from politics into co-operation and trade unionism, there was nothing to sustain such an international centre. Harney and his friends did their best to keep the Society alive by publishing numerous manifestos, by holding meetings on revolutionary anniversaries, and by collecting money for refugees in want, but by 1852 the Fraternal Democrats were forced finally to disband. Harney himself gradually dropped out of active politics.

This work was carried on, however, by Ernest Jones. After he had served a prison sentence for Chartist activity, Jones tried to rally some of the old revolutionary elements around him. Though he had little success in this, he became the chairman of a new body called the International Committee, on which sat representatives of the refugee groups in London. This organization, like the Fraternal Democrats, issued a number of manifestos and called commemorative gatherings. But its outlook was much more confused. Deprived of the chance to do really effective political work, the exiles and their English associates fell back on empty rhetoric. Their public statements were full of revolutionary abstractions and vague but rolling phrases. The slogans of 1848 were repeated on every possible occasion without any apparent understanding that times had changed.

In April 1856 a delegation of Paris workers arrived in London to discuss the formation of a Universal League of Workmen which would unite the workers of all countries against international capital, and thereby secure their social emancipation. The Frenchmen, strongly influenced by the ideas of Louis Blanc and Proudhon, wished to impose a levy on twenty million workers throughout Europe, using the money to set up a network of producers' and consumers' co-operatives which, by their superior efficiency, would drive private capitalism out of business. Among those who took up this utopian project was the former Chartist leader Bronterre O'Brien.

Of course, the scheme was a failure, but it had a stimulating effect on the International Committee, which issued a manifesto stating that it proposed to expand into an international association open to members in all countries, with separate local committees in as many cities as possible. It would seek to recruit individual members who would be entitled to a vote at both national and international congresses

of the organization. This proposal, like that for the Universal
League, came to very little, though the International Association apparently succeeded in making contact with supporters
in Europe and in America.

But it is worth noting that the form of the organization
was almost an exact anticipation of the structure of the
First International. In fact, when another French delegation attended a meeting in London in September 1864,
from which the initiative came for the formation of the
First International, this was nothing particularly unusual. For,
all through the years in which socialism made little headway
as a mass movement, there had still been meetings called to
affirm the idea of international proletarian solidarity. Only two
years elapsed between the dissolution of the organization led
by Jones and the establishment of the new and more successful
International Working Men's Association. To its founders,
indeed, the latter probably appeared as the direct continuation
of the pioneering work of Harney and Jones. But the First
International was far more effective than anything they ever
did, though it owed much to their efforts.

The reason for this is not hard to find. By the 'sixties the
recovery of the movement on the Continent made it possible
to set up an international organization which could secure
genuine backing. The predecessors of the International,
struggling against the stream, were primarily collections of
sectarian refugees and old Chartist leaders who increasingly
lost touch with the workers they were trying to lead. But the
International did not depend very much upon these people.
It was able to tap the new forces that were emerging in Europe
and, for a time, to weld them together for common purposes.
It therefore became a body which was far more mature and
influential than anything which had appeared up to that
point.

Nothing better illustrates this change than the character
of the English trade union leaders, who played a large part in
the formation and work of the International. While they did
not possess the fire of the old stalwarts like Harney and Jones,
they faithfully reflected the new mood of the working-class.
They had little use for inflammatory speeches: they were more

concerned with solving the immediate problems created by the rapid and enormous expansion of British industry. The hunger and unemployment of the Chartist days had given way to a serious labour shortage. Apart from the demands of the factories and the great construction enterprises like the development of the railways, millions had emigrated.

During this period trade unionism had taken a strong hold— though it was now organized on a craft instead of an industrial basis—and had thrown up leaders like Applegarth, Allan, Odger and Cremer. These men were prepared to join in demonstrations in favour of Polish independence or the abolition of slavery in the United States, but one of the main reasons for their interest in international working-class action was their desire to exert some control on the numbers of foreign workers who were arriving in England, attracted by the industrial boom. The trade unions, which were reaping the benefit of labour scarcity, were anxious to prevent cheap foreign labour being used to drive down the rates they had so laboriously managed to push up. Odger and the others had taken steps to get in touch with French workers in 1863. In 1864 they helped to found the International.

In France events were moving in much the same direction. Working-class discontent increased considerably after the economic crisis of 1857 and the war against Austria in 1859, and socialist propaganda began to produce results. The most influential group was that which supported Proudhon, at this time in exile in Belgium. Though its programme included the usual demands for mutual credit associations and denied the value of strikes and political activity, the events of the early 'sixties gradually convinced the Proudhonists that the workers should nominate their own candidates for the elections to the legislative assembly, though, on the theoretical side, they still kept to the original programme. Proudhon himself was won over to this point of view just before his death. The Proudhonists, moreover, were strongly represented in the delegation of French workers which, under official auspices, visited London for the Exhibition of 1862 and made contact with English and German working-class leaders there.

At this time two things were happening which drew the

French and English workers together. The first was the American Civil War, which had a profound effect on the entire economic life of Europe. Committees to help the workers who were unemployed as a result of the dislocation of the textile trade were set up in both France and England and communicated frequently with each other. The working-class was also in enthusiastic support of the Union armies, even when this support ran counter to their economic interests. The second was the Polish insurrection. In the agitation to support the insurgent Poles, the French and English workers took a large share. Again there was contact between the two movements on a matter of common interest.

All this preliminary work culminated in the meeting which was held on September 28, 1864, to receive the reply of the French workers to the fraternal message addressed to them almost a year before by Odger and the other English leaders. Tolain, speaking for the French delegation, successfully urged that an international organization of workers should be immediately set up.

But the committee that was appointed to further this project had no definite instructions. It consisted, moreover, of several national sections which had no similarity in outlook. The English representatives included former Chartists and trade unionists; the Poles were concerned with little but their own national problems; Mazzini, the republican, led the Italians; Marx, like the other Germans with him, was an old member of the Communist League. When efforts to produce an agreed constitution failed, the task of making another draft was given to Marx, who, by making a number of concessions on points which he considered immaterial, managed to steer his version through the committee. The First International was born.

The Inaugural Address of the International was a brilliant effort to put the communist outlook in a form which would be acceptable to a number of working-class organizations, each of which was in an early and different stage of development. Marx, on the basis of his exhaustive study of labour conditions and the structure of capitalist society, put forward a number of propositions on which he believed that all these groups could unite. Reviewing the changes that had taken place since 1848, Marx insisted that the gulf between the workers and the bourgeoisie was widening in spite of the great increase in wealth. He criticized the idea of superseding private enterprise by co-operative production on a national scale, pointing out that the ruling class would use its political power to prevent such usurpation of its economic privileges. The first duty of the workers, therefore, was to form political labour parties all over the world, as a means to the conquest of power by and for themselves. Lacking a national and an international organization, the workers could achieve nothing; united, they could overthrow the capitalists and transfer the control of production to society as a whole.

Though each section of the committee was inclined to take a different interpretation of these points, Marx was able to incorporate them into the Constitution of the International, as well as express them in the *Inaugural Address*. He did this so brilliantly that some of his phrases were literally transcribed into the programmes of many later working-class parties, particularly in Germany.

The technical preparations completed, the provisional leadership was anxious to hold the first congress and get on with the work of the International. But things were not quite so simple as that. Though the movement was reviving all over the Continent, there was still a great deal of political and organizational confusion. It was clear that before the International could begin to lead the workers of the world it was going to have some difficulty in persuading them to unite.

CHAPTER VII

THE FIRST INTERNATIONAL

IN the course of its comparatively short life the International became the terror of the ruling classes of Europe, though, in spite of its considerable achievements, it was never as powerful as they imagined. It was not a disciplined and unified body which unquestioningly accepted the revolutionary doctrines of Marx, but a federal organization which only survived with difficulty a series of factional disputes on both theoretical and practical issues. All the same, Marx was the dominant influence in it, and most of the time he managed to carry a majority of delegates with him in the controversies provoked by the followers of Proudhon, and later by Bakunin and the anarchists. He succeeded in holding the International together because he understood how far and how fast he could move the limited forces at its disposal. He was not prepared to compromise on anything he believed to be a matter of principle, and he was a resolute opponent of the utopian and extremist schemes put forward by some groups in the International on the grounds that they would quickly lead to its complete disintegration.

While Marx was an expert tactician, however, he was able to do very little about the failure of the International to strike any strong roots in Germany. He was personally concerned with this problem, since it arose in part from the split between the group which looked to him for leadership and that which supported Ferdinand Lassalle, the founder of the German workers' movement.

Lassalle had worked with Marx and Engels in the Rhineland during the revolution of 1848, and was one of the first persons to study and adopt their philosophy of historical materialism. When his friends were forced into exile, Lassalle remained in Germany and spent most of the next ten years in prosecuting a sensational lawsuit. Though he kept in touch with the exiles, he did almost nothing in the way of politics.

His relations with Marx cooled gradually, but there was an open breach between the two of them over Lassalle's attitude to the French war against Austria in 1859. He ardently desired the national unity of Germany—indeed his rationalism was as powerful a motive of his political actions as his socialism—and to secure it he was prepared to enlist the support of the Prussian ruling class. Austria, he believed, was the main obstacle, and therefore he hoped for a French victory.

Marx and Engels, however, insisted that the unification of Germany by Prussia would be worse than no unity at all. They saw a danger of Russian intervention on the side of France, and in that event hoped for a revolutionary war of the German peoples in which the progressive elements would come to the fore and both unify and democratize the loose confederation. Whatever the merits of the diplomatic argument, it revealed a difference in outlook that was to become increasingly important. If, in 1859, Lassalle thought that official Prussia was the one force which could effectively unify Germany, it was only logical that he should later be ready to believe that Bismarck could be persuaded to introduce the social changes which the middle-class seemed incapable of achieving. The degree to which the German workers' movement was influenced by nationalist sentiments is worth noting at this stage. For, in the next three generations, the readiness of large sections of the movement to subordinate their "class", or socialist, aspirations to the interests of a United Fatherland was frequently decisive. Lassalle's blend of chauvinism and social progress became an attractive though dangerous formula. It was borrowed by intelligent conservatives outside Germany: it was applied successfully inside Germany at every critical moment, from Bismarck's time until the rise of National Socialism.

From the beginning of his agitation in 1862 Lassalle bitterly opposed the liberal groups with which he had previously been associated. To a committee which had been set up in Leipzig to organize a congress of workers Lassalle addressed his famous *Open Letter*. In this he urged the formation of an independent working-class party. The workers, he said, could look for no improvement of their conditions under the existing system; for the "iron law of wages" proved that if higher wages were secured by one group of workers the wages of other groups would inevitably fall. He argued that the solution of the social problem lay in the creation of co-operative associations by a State based on universal suffrage, in which all workmen would receive the full product of their labour. This programme won over the Leipzig committee completely, and in May 1863 the Universal German Working Men's Association was founded, with the one immediate aim of universal suffrage. For the next two years Lassalle travelled through Germany, speaking to great audiences of workers and laying the basis of a national proletarian movement for the first time. In August 1864 he was killed in a duel.

Lassalle was as vain as he was able. Much has been written about this erratic and brilliant personality which emphasizes his weakness, but none of it can obscure his achievement in reviving socialist agitation in Germany after years of apathy and inaction. Unfortunately, there was no general agreement that he had set the working-class movement going again in the right direction. Almost at once Marx and Engels joined issue with the Lassallians. While they agreed with the demand for universal suffrage, they refused to endorse Lassalle's naïve suggestion that, independent of anything else, it could rapidly place all power in the hands of the workers. Lassalle, they said, overlooked the important part that trade unions played in the class-struggle. Though he claimed to be a follower of Marx, he urged the establishment of co-operative associations as competitors with private enterprise within the framework of the capitalist State, whereas Marx continually insisted that the conquest of power and the elimination of capitalist production was a prerequisite of successful co-operation on a national scale. But, above all, the quarrel was due to a dispute about the attitude that socialists should adopt towards the progressive middle-class parties. Marx had no illusions about the liberals, but he believed that the working-class should support them whenever they came into conflict with Bismarck and Prussian reaction. Lassalle, however, who bitterly denounced the liberal democrats, was unable to see that the ruling-class of

Prussia, the Junkers who were represented by Bismarck, was the real and most dangerous opponent of the weak socialist movement.

While Marx was much criticized at the time for his refusal to have anything to do with Lassalle's political activity, he was quite justified by facts which came to light many years later when the secret correspondence between Lassalle and Bismarck was published. Lassalle hoped that Bismarck would make far-reaching concessions, would permit the workers to organize freely, would give them the vote and assist them to form co-operative associations. In return, he was prepared to support Bismarck's diplomatic adventures and his campaign against the liberals.

This policy would certainly have made the workers' movement a cat's-paw of the most reactionary force in German politics. It was the main reason for the breach between the Lassallians and the Marxists. The latter's suspicions were only increased when, in the war of 1866 against Austria, Bismarck introduced universal suffrage in order to secure the support of the workers. This war, if he had lived to see it, would have been greeted enthusiastically by Lassalle, for it was waged to exclude Austria from the German Confederation and to secure the hegemony of Prussia over all the other German States.

After the death of Lassalle a serious split developed between Schweitzer, the editor of the party organ *The Social-Democrat*, and Wilhelm Liebknecht, an old and close associate of Marx and Engels. Schweitzer wished to go on working along the same lines as Lassalle, since he believed that the independent workers' movement would be crushed if it tried to oppose the liberals and Bismarck simultaneously. When he printed a series of articles which could justifiably be interpreted as a eulogy of Bismarck's policy, Liebknecht resigned his position on the paper. After this split there was no question of the Lassallians affiliating to an International in which Marx played a leading part.

The Lassallians, all the same, did not have a monopoly of the German working-class organizations. There was a large number of groups which had been originally formed as offshoots of the Liberal Progressive Party. Most of these were formed from Saxon and South-German workers who disliked the growing ascendancy of Prussia. Under the leadership of Liebknecht and August Bebel, the two most prominent figures in the early days of the mass Social-Democratic Party, these workers were gradually won over to Marxist socialism. The union of these groups, at its congress in Nuremberg in 1868, decided to join the International. The next year, at the Eisenach Congress, the Social-Democratic Working Men's Party was founded. Thanks to Bismarck's introduction of universal suffrage, both the Lassallians and the Eisenachers were able to secure a few seats in the Diet of the North-German Confederation.

When the International at last held its inaugural congress at Geneva in 1866, however, the only Germans present were the representatives of the *émigré* circles in Switzerland and England. Marx himself, who was finishing the first volume of *Capital*, was too busy and sick to attend. Instead, he prepared an elaborate brief for the delegation which travelled out from London. It was soon needed. Supporters of Proudhon were in a majority among the French at the congress, and they made a determined effort to capture the International. They wanted it to declare its opposition to strikes and trade unions and its support of co-operative production based upon the free supply of credit. The English and Germans would have none of this mutualist programme. Basing themselves on the brief supplied by Marx, but making verbal concessions to the French, who controlled about a third of the congress, they succeeded in defeating most of the Proudhonist motions, including one that sought to confine membership of the International to manual workers—which would have excluded Marx, among others.

The final decisions of the Geneva Congress, reached after a series of chaotic debates, were a considerable victory for Marx and those who stood with him. While they did not commit the International to socialism, most of the tactical demands upon which Marx hoped to unite its various sections were at this point included in the official programme. In spite of the opposition of the powerful group of French delegates, the

E

congress carried resolutions demanding protective labour legislation and a shorter working day, and insisted that trade unions were essential as the organizational centres for the workers, whose only strength lay in their numbers and their unity, against the powers of capitalist society.

During the next two years the influence of the International increased rapidly. The Lausanne Congress of 1867, and that held at Brussels in the following year, made it quite clear that the International was a socialist body. Though compromises with the French followers of Proudhon were still necessary, they were gradually won over to the socialist argument for collective ownership of the land, transport and communication facilities.

By the time of the Brussels Congress the International was sufficiently important to attract a good deal of attention from the European Press. *The Times*, which devoted four leading articles to the proceedings at Brussels, wrote: "It is not a mere improvement that is contemplated, but nothing less than a regeneration, and that not of one nation only, but of mankind. This is certainly the most extensive aim ever contemplated by any institution, with the exception, perhaps, of the Christian Church."

The International was not always discussed in such moderate terms. It was more usually denounced as the sinister force behind every workmen's agitation or revolutionary movement. But its prestige was based rather on the potentialities of the cause it championed than on a realistic assessment of its strength. While it gave support to strikes in Paris and assisted the English trade unions by preventing the importation of cheap labour, it exercised only a very loose control over its affiliated sections in every European country. At no time, moreover, did it possess anything but the most meagre financial resources for the enormous amount of work it tried to carry on.

The International was never free from serious internal dissensions. Up to the Basle Congress in 1869 the Proudhonists were the chief opponents of the line followed by the leadership. At that congress, however, Bakunin and the anarchists took their place, and the International became a forum for the bitter factional struggle between Bakunin and the General Council, which supported Marx.

Michael Bakunin, who spent the greater part of his life as an exile from his native Russia, was one of the most extraordinary figures in the nineteenth century. Like Marx and Engels, he was influenced by the Young Hegelian group in Germany during the 'forties. In 1848, after he had associated himself with the attempt of the exiles in Paris to form a revolutionary legion to invade Germany, he fought in the Bohemian and Saxon insurrections. Arrested at Dresden, he was handed over to the Russian police and imprisoned. A few years later he escaped from Siberia and returned to Europe by way of Japan and America. Though he met Marx in London during 1864 and promised his support for the International, he spent the next four years in Italy and Switzerland, organizing his own revolutionary movement. In 1868 he founded the International Social-Democratic Alliance.

The Alliance was dominated by Bakunin, who believed that Marx overestimated the importance of the working-class. Still thinking in terms of the conditions of 1848, he insisted that the intelligentzia, especially the students, was a much more revolutionary element in society than the uneducated workers, whose energies were taken up with the struggle for their daily bread. The Alliance was a conspiratorial organization, in the tradition of the old secret societies. It expected its members to be atheists who would wage war on religion and the State with equal resolution. But, in spite of its predeliction for revolutionary phrases, it was not based on a consistent socialist programme. Bakunin, anxious not to frighten away potential supporters, at this time confined himself to vague demands for political and economic equality.

When theAlliance asked for affiliation to the International as a separate body, retaining its own constitution and programme, this request was refused by the General Council, which was already suspicious of Bakunin's intentions. Its members were admitted only after the Alliance was officially disbanded. All the same, their loyalty to the International was questionable. Marx had well-founded suspicions that Bakunin had entered the International only to capture it for his own ends. Both of them sought the destruction of bourgeois society by a social revolution.

But Bakunin, who had no faith at all in the political organization of the working-class, regarded Marx as an obstacle to the insurrection which, he believed, could be carried out only by the alliance of the revolutionary intellectuals and the most wretched and depressed elements among the workers. Within the International he accused Marx and the General Council of seeking to lead the movement towards the new tyranny of bureaucratic State socialism instead of struggling for a new society in which there would no longer be a division between the rulers and the ruled, and in which men would live in real freedom as members of a federation of self-governing associations.

Though Bakunin secured considerable support at the Basle Congress, it was only later that his anarchist opposition became a serious challenge to the policy and position of the General Council. In the next year there were other things to occupy the attention of the International. It had already discussed the danger of a Franco-Prussian war at its Brussels Congress, and, denouncing all war as systematic murder, had urged that the workers should declare a general strike against it.

In July 1870, without much warning, war actually began between France and Germany, and the workers of each country were unable to do anything to prevent it. The International had to be content with issuing a proclamation written by Marx in which both Bismarck and Napoleon the Third were blamed for the disaster, and the collapse of the French régime was prophesied. In a few weeks France was, in fact, defeated and Napoleon himself captured. A republic was thereupon declared in Paris and a new government set up to continue the war as best it could. In a second manifesto, written on behalf of the International, Marx urged the German workers to demand an honourable peace and the recognition of the French Republic; the French proletariat was advised to keep a close watch on the vacillating and untrustworthy middle-class republicans. Above all, Marx declared that Bismarck's annexation of Alsace-Lorraine would only lead to another war in which France and Russia would be allied against Germany.

Paris capitulated late in January 1871. Though the armistice terms permitted the National Guard to retain its arms, the new government at Versailles, which was dominated by the reactionary parties, was far more concerned to deprive the radical population of Paris of its weapons than to protect the national interests of France against the excessive demands made by Bismarck. On March 18, when an unsuccessful attempt was made to seize the guns of the National Guard, Paris rose in revolt. On March 26 the Commune was elected. It survived until the end of May, when the defences of Paris were broken down and thousands of workers butchered in the streets by the Versailles army.

The Commune was a spontaneous rising by the Paris workers, who were disgusted with the treachery, corruption and exploitation that characterized their rulers. Though the International was universally charged with responsibility for the revolt, it was unable to give either effective guidance or practical assistance to besieged Paris. Even inside the city the members of its Paris section, who sat on the Council of the Commune, were outnumbered by the supporters of the veteran revolutionary Blanqui, who was still alive but who was prevented from entering Paris.

Nevertheless, the International willingly assumed the task of defending the motives and actions of the communards against an unprecedented campaign of abuse and misrepresentation. Marx was well aware that the leaders of the Commune were guilty of serious errors—some of which had accelerated its defeat—but he did not allow these to blind him to its real achievement. The Commune, he insisted in his brilliant commentary *The Civil War in France*, was the first occasion in history on which the working-class had seized power. It was the prototype of the proletarian dictatorship which would one day undertake the transition from capitalist to communist society. It had abolished both the standing army and the police, and given arms to the masses. It had begun to break the power of the clergy, the allies of the rulers of France, by expropriating their property. It had intended to provide free and universal education. And, finally, it had broken the old bureaucracy of State servants by making all public officials subject to election or deposition at any time, and by fixing their salary at a figure no higher than that of a skilled workman. The Commune lived for only six weeks, but, said Marx, it "will be commemorated for ever as the glorious herald of a new society". It had a lasting effect, not only upon the generation of workers which had witnessed it but also upon the whole development of European socialism.

After the defeat of the Commune, however, the International began to disintegrate. At the same time as it had to devote a good deal of energy to assist the numerous communard refugees, it was faced with a campaign of repression in a number of important countries. This would have been less serious if the various sections of the International had presented a united front against their persecutors, but, on the contrary, the internal feud between Marx and Bakunin had been intensified by the experiences of the Commune, the anarchists claiming that these justified their belief in a spontaneous revolt which could abolish the old State and establish universal freedom without any need for the intervening period of proletarian dictatorship on which the Marxists insisted. The French labour movement was paralysed for some years by the repression which followed the Commune. In Germany both Liebknecht and Bebel were imprisoned. They had refused to follow the Lassallians in voting for war credits in 1870, they had protested against the annexation of Alsace-Lorraine, and they had declared their solidarity with the Paris Commune.

Though the followers of Lassalle had their share of persecution, the militancy of the Eisenach party, which alone was affiliated to the International, involved it in serious trouble. In England, for reasons which are discussed below, the trade unions withdrew their support from the General Council. Thus in the three most advanced industrial countries, on whose workers the International had depended for its chief support, its influence dwindled rapidly.

A fair measure of the relative importance of the working-class movement in each country in the days when the International was at its zenith is provided by the number

of representatives that each section had on the General
Council—though many of these were exiles in London and
were nominal rather than effective representatives. There
were twenty from England, fifteen from France, seven from
Germany, two from Switzerland and Hungary, and only one
each from Poland, Belgium, Ireland, Denmark and Italy. The
events of 1871 changed all that. At the private conference
which met in London that year the International could not
muster even as many delegates as there had once been members
of the General Council.

But the International did not collapse at once. There was
another congress at the Hague in 1872 at which the anarchists
were formally expelled, and it was decided to remove the seat
of the General Council to New York, where it remained until
the International was finally liquidated in 1876. In its last years
the anarchist organizations, which had been reformed into the
Alliance, became increasingly powerful and outrivalled the
International.

As the possibilities of effective action on the part of the
International diminished, so the personal and theoretical
disputes between the two rival movements became more
bitter. In Spain and Italy, both of them backward countries
without a large proletariat, Bakunin's doctrines found
support. In 1873 there were risings under anarchist leadership in Barcelona, Seville, Cadiz and Cartagena, which were
suppressed only with difficulty. Everywhere Bakunin was
gaining ground at the expense of Marx.

But the decline of the organization was not primarily
due to the disruptive intrigues of the anarchists, as Marx
and Engels believed at the time. The truth was that conditions were no longer suitable for the kind of work that
the International sought to do. The working-class movement
was not developing at a steady rate or following the same
course in each country. On the contrary, there were important
and growing divergences. In places such as Spain and Italy,
where industry was in its infancy and the only possible form of
political activity was conspiracy followed by insurrection, the
Marxist insistence on the necessity of forming trade unions
and an independent workers' party had little appeal.

The workers in such nations, moreover, still retained much of the individualism of the peasant and readily listened to the anarchist ideas of Proudhon and Bakunin. Marx, though he always understood that the working-class had to adapt its tactics to the different social and economic circumstances of each country, placed the greatest emphasis, during the formative period of the International, on the problems which were common to the workers of all capitalist societies—the demand for shorter hours or.for freedom of organization—and preferred to leave the more specific national problems open until the parties fostered by the International were more mature.

After 1871 the position of the working-class parties varied so much from one country to another that they could not afford to concentrate on general issues at the expense of the local and particular difficulties they had to face. At first Marx sought to check the decline of the International by strengthening the authority of the General Council, but the more he tried to control the constituent sections from a common centre, the more he hastened the process of disintegation. Gradually he came to realize that the International had outlived its usefulness and that the socialist movement had entered a new phase in its development.

The life of the International was short and, in spite of some limited practical successes, it was never much more than a propagandist body. Yet it laid the foundation of the modern socialist movement. It was the platform from which Marx was able to speak with such effect that Marxism became the gospel of millions of workers in the next fifty years. It finally destroyed the belief that the workers could contract out of the miseries they endured in capitalist society by setting up co-operative communities, without any need for a political or economic struggle against the employers or the State they dominated.

And, by continually insisting that the working-class must seek its own salvation by the seizure of political power and the liquidation of capitalist enterprise, it gave a tremendous stimulus to the formation of independent workers' parties. These parties, insofar as they were based upon Marxism, were also spurred on by the conviction that they were identifying themselves with the course of history and that they would ultimately triumph, whatever obstacles they temporarily encountered. Just as Marx transformed the theory of socialism, so the International was largely responsible for the conversion of the movement from a collection of disunited and virtually utopian sects into a number of realistic and well-established parties. After the defeat of the Paris Commune, as the prospect of revolution faded, each of these parties went its own way, adapting the basic principles of socialism to the political conditions of its own country.

CHAPTER VIII

THE REVIVAL IN BRITAIN

THE character of the labour and socialist movements in Britain has always differed radically from that of their European counterparts. They have been, in their modern expression, empirical movements which acquired theories slowly and almost haphazardly, rather than movements which were created to advance a definite ideology. Their history, therefore, is as much a history of organizations as of theories. Long before socialism became an effective political force on the Continent the English workers were familiar with the socialist doctrines of Robert Owen and his contemporaries, and in the course of the Chartist agitation they had even created a mass revolutionary party of their own. But in the middle of the nineteenth century, just as socialism was beginning to make some headway in Europe, the English working-class abandoned it and turned instead to trade unionism, to consumers' co-operation and to the support of the middle-class reformers. The break with the past was complete.

For almost thirty years, from 1850 to 1880, socialism played no part of any consequence in the labour movement of this country. The experiences of the Chartist period were forgotten. Marxism, which secured an increasing influence among the workers of Europe, was either totally ignored or else dismissed, by the few who took the trouble to notice it at all, as an obsolete and untenable philosophy which had no relevance to the conditions in England. Although, at the turn of the century, there was a socialist revival, both the structure and outlook of the Labour Party that eventually emerged from it were a reflection of the political tranquillity and prosperity of Britain. The constitutional reform of society rather than the revolutionary seizure of power became the objective of British socialism.

It was not accidental that this period of comparatively peaceful and non-political development coincided with the years of British industrial supremacy. Though the improvement in the standard of life of the working-class in this period has often been exaggerated, there is no doubt that the workers, especially the skilled artisans, did share in the wealth that was pouring into Britain, and that this was a material factor in reconciling them to the capitalist system. They were forced, it is true, into some bitter and protracted industrial disputes. But, on these occasions, they were always at pains to point out that their quarrel was not with employers as a class but with particular individuals or groups which refused to grant the unions the recognition they regarded as their due or the limited and specific demands they made for wage advances, shorter hours or better working conditions. Until about 1880 there was no suggestion that the system itself should be challenged. On the contrary, some of the trade union leaders were as enthusiastic as the employers in their eulogies of free enterprise.

The history of the British Labour movement after 1850, therefore, is primarily the history of trade unionism. But these unions were very different from their Owenite predecessors, the remnants of which struggled without much success to keep going under the new conditions. Even before 1850 there were signs that a fresh outlook was developing among some of the trade unions, but the first real change dates from the foundation of the Amalgamated Society of Engineers by the fusion of a number of smaller unions in 1851. This was the first of a whole series of unions which grew up in the 'sixties and 'seventies, catering almost entirely for the skilled workers, which sought to minimize rather than provoke conflict with the employers, to negotiate rather than to strike, to regulate the supply of labour to their trades, to centralize authority and control of union finances, and to provide considerable sickness and unemployment benefits for their members.

This new outlook was not accepted at once or without some opposition—even the A.S.E. was forced to retain the old Owenite demand for the foundation of co-operative colonies in its constitution—but, under the leadership of a small group known as the Junta, the success of these "new model" unions was such that they became the most stable and powerful section of the movement. Some of their leaders, men like Odger and Applegarth, for instance, were willing to sit on the General Council of the International, which for a short time was the effective centre of working-class organization in this country, but they took little interest in the theoretical polemics of that body. For them it was an organization which helped to prevent the importation of cheap foreign labour into Britain and a means through which they could express their sympathy with oppressed democrats or national movements on the Continent.

It is doubtful if they understood at first exactly what the programme of the International meant. In any case, they severed their connection with it after Marx had openly championed the execrated Paris Commune, when it was clear the International had no more practical help to offer them. They had always refused to dissociate themselves from the radical section of the middle-class and, in spite of the efforts that Marx made to persuade them to put forward a distinctive proletarian programme during the renewed campaign for an extension of the suffrage in the 'sixties, they took the trade unions into an alliance with the Radical reform movement. They justified this decision partly on the grounds that it was a waste of the workers' money to conduct an independent agitation and partly by insisting that there was only a difference of degree and not of principle between their views and those of reformers like Cobden and John Bright.

This partnership was only the beginning of a long period in which the working-class played no separate role in British politics. It was drawn into the struggle between the Liberals and the Conservatives, and it was left to individual workers to choose which of the two traditional parties they would support. Though the unions continually declared that they had no interest in politics, this only meant that they saw no need to organize their members as a class with aims quite distinct from those of other sections of the community. Whenever legal judgments or new laws threatened to withhold the right of free combination, there was an attempt to send working-class representatives to Parliament, but it was never intended that these representatives should form the nucleus of a socialist party. On the contrary, they were put forward to ensure that the workers should have someone to speak for them in Parliament, just as the doctors, lawyers, landlords and other groups had spokesmen there who looked after their special interests. In fact, when the idea that the trade unions should sponsor their own party was raised, it found no more bitter antagonists than among the working-men who had been elected as Liberals.

The working-class leaders of this type—though there were important exceptions among the textile workers' and the miners' leaders—became increasingly identified with the outlook of the employers and of the Manchester school of economics, which taught that the less interference there was with the operations of free enterprise, the greater the prosperity of capitalist and worker alike. These men publicly rejoiced in the harmony they had created between master and labourer. They were respectable. On occasion they were willing to trade the interests of the men they led for the friendship of their Tory and Liberal friends. As early as 1871, when Applegarth stood as a candidate for the London School Board—this was only a few months after he had resigned from the International—his Conservative opponent withdrew and donated twenty pounds to his election fund.

This same man was the secretary of the London Master Builders' Association, the organization which Applegarth and his union had spent years in fighting. It was not that these men, as a rule, were personally corrupt in the sense that they were bought by the offer of money or office. They were convinced of the values of Liberalism. Their actions reflected the attitude of the skilled workers, who believed that they had more to gain by peaceful collaboration than by conflict with an expanding economic system. This outlook was encouraged by a large number of organizations which, agreeing that reforms were necessary, argued that they could be secured by persuasion. The more the workmen displayed their thrift, their moderation and their self-discipline, it was said, the more likely it was that they would be considered worthy of the franchise, of higher wages and shorter hours. They were urged to devote the energies that might otherwise have been diverted into politics to religious duties, to the consumers' co-operatives which were developing rapidly throughout the country, and to the extension of the friendly society functions of their unions.

It is also necessary to take account of the difference between the English ruling-class and its European counterparts. It was more intelligent and flexible. It understood that much was to be gained if it sought to conciliate instead of to suppress the organizations of the working-class. It was able, when the demand for social change became too strong to ignore, to satisfy it by limited concessions at the critical moment. This was possible, of course, because the rulers of England seemed secure against any challenge and because they were sufficiently rich and successful to afford sections of the workers a share in their prosperity. Class differences were also less rigid in England, and the strong Noncomformist tradition cut across classes and thus prevented a sharp cleavage along either religious or social lines.

Too much stress, however, can be laid on the benefits which the working-class as a whole secured from the policy of conciliation pursued by its leaders and on the tolerance of the British employers towards trade unionism. In fact, the rise in living standards in the last twenty years of the nineteenth century was due as much to a steady decline in commodity prices as to wage increases, which in most trades were erratic and slow. The unions, moreover, had to fight hard for recognition in spite of their lack of militancy. The Liberals, by an Act of 1871, gave them legal protection for their funds. They managed, in return for supporting the Tories in the election of 1874, to obtain a further Act which recognized their right to strike. But their position was never too sure and, as we shall see, they were eventually driven into independent political action by a renewed threat to their legal standing.

In the period of prosperity that lasted to the end of the 'seventies, the unions—backed by the votes of the workers who had been enfranchised in 1867—secured a number of successes. The engineers won the nine-hour day, the miners the safety provisions of the Mines Act of 1872, and the factory workers an improvement in their working conditions by the Act of 1875. But the advances made by the unions themselves were almost wiped out by the disastrous economic crisis that started in 1879. The crisis, which was largely due to increasing foreign competition, hit both industry and agriculture severely. It produced a radical change in the nature of British capitalism, for from this crisis dates the appearance of two phenomena which were henceforth to be inseparable from it—imperialism and mass unemployment.

Until Disraeli, by a stroke of political genius, had identified the glory of empire with the fortunes of the Tory Party by making Queen Victoria the Empress of India, nobody in England had realized the value of the overseas possessions. But, by the economic slump of 1879, the challenge of foreign rivals to British industrial supremacy began, among other things, to take the form of an increasingly bitter struggle between the Powers for colonial territories. This imperialist scramble, moreover, was accompanied by a stimulated wave of jingoism which did something to offset social criticism provoked by successive revelations of the conditions of the poor and unemployed. During the 'seventies there was an upsurge of the Radical movement, led by Joseph Chamberlain and Charles Dilke—who at one time seemed likely to launch a full-blooded republican campaign—and there is no doubt that this Radical propaganda played a considerable part in preparing the way for the later development of a distinctively British form of socialism, which finally took form in the Labour Party.

After the crisis of 1879 there was a revival of socialist activity in Britain. Henry Hyndman, a wealthy Radical who had become disillusioned with Liberalism, founded the Democratic Federation in 1881, later reorganizing it as the Social-Democratic Federation. Hyndman converted the S.D.F. to a form of Marxist socialism and began agitating for the creation of a large working-class party. At first the S.D.F. spent its efforts on the unemployed, believing they offered a good field for revolutionary activity, launching a campaign of socialist propaganda which lasted until 1914. It rivalled the achievements of Robert Blatchford, the author of *Merrie England*, which sold a million copies, and his supporters grouped round the paper, *Clarion*, as the source of pioneering socialist education for many thousands of workers. But the S.D.F., for all its efforts, was never able to rally a significant body of working-class support behind it. Its work in the depression years, however, was not entirely fruitless.

At the end of the 'eighties a small group of able young trade unionists, who had been won over to socialism by the Federation, set to work to organize the unskilled workers. Led by Tom Mann and John Burns, this "new unionism", as it was called, won some striking victories, especially in the great dock strike in 1889 in London. It differed from the craft unionism of the skilled tradesmen in its insistence on a militant industrial policy and in its endorsement of a programme of moderate social reforms such as the right to work, the eight-hour day and the municipal owner-ship of public utilities, but it was equally unwilling to accept the revolutionary Marxism preached by the Federation.

There are a number of reasons why the Federation remained a small sectarian body. The most important was the reformist outlook which dominated a majority of the workers. It was little use talking revolution and class-war to a proletariat which was convinced that its interests lay in peaceful acceptance of capitalism. The most prosperous and best educated workers, as we have seen, were completely dominated by the ideas of class-harmony so assiduously preached by their leaders, employers and a host of religous and political reformers.

The Federation, moreover, had very little conception of the importance of trade unionism, which it regarded as a reaction-ary force diverting the workers from the political struggle for socialism. Instead of participating in and guiding the day-to-day activities of the working-class, as Marx had urged ever since the publication of the *Communist Manifesto*, it put forward a peculiarly dogmatic and inflexible version of Marxism. It was not surprising that the workers failed to see what relation this involved philosophy had to their everyday problems. The leaders of the Federation themselves had only a very limited acquaintance with the work of Marx and Engels, and as often as not they only partially understood the fragments they did read. They had no sense of tactics. Though some of them were able leaders of the unemployed, they failed to relate their Marxist ideology effectively to the mass movements they were seeking to create. The Federation was also weakened by internal disputes, particularly in its early days, when it served as a political home for anarchists, radical reformers, revolution-ary Marxists and anti-parliamentary socialists alike.

As early as 1884 part of the Federation split away to form the Socialist League. This break had the approval of Engels

—Marx had died in the previous year—and Eleanor Aveling, one of the daughters of Marx, was one of the leading figures in the League. But the League was not even as homogeneous as the Federation, in which many of the self-styled Marxists remained. Some of the League members had broken away because they disliked and distrusted Hyndman, some because they thought that there was no point in such a weak organization trying to act as a proper political party, and others because they had no faith at all in the value of parliamentary institutions or of palliative reforms. For a short time in the 'eighties the League carried on an independent agitation, but it passed more and more under the control of its anarchist wing and eventually the Marxists and parliamentary socialists abandoned it and rejoined the Federation.

Although the League was even less successful than the Federation, it had in William Morris a leader who was one of the most remarkable figures in the history of socialism in Britain. Morris, who was an artist and a poet of extraordinary ability, was led to socialism by his hatred of the squalor and ugliness of industrial capitalist society. He wanted to make life rich and beautiful for all men, and believed that this would be possible only when all things were shared in common and men worked for the joy of creative effort instead of selling their bodies and their souls to a master bent on profit at any price. He hated a social system which made art and culture inaccessible to all save those with wealth, and at the same time put such a premium on the pursuit of riches that all standards of taste and value were corrupted. Until the victory of socialism enabled man to realize his full spiritual and intellectual capacities, he was convinced, life for the majority would be narrow, sordid and colourless. His romantic vision of a socialist England, *News from Nowhere*, was one of the finest of all utopias, written in an imaginative and glowing style that has lost none of its appeal.

But Morris was neither a dreamer nor a dilettante. He passionately desired to make his utopia grow out of the poverty and the hideous industrialism he saw all around him. No task was too big or too petty for him to tackle. He was ready to sacrifice his energies and his money alike to the socialist cause. He wrote books, poems and articles for the movement; he lectured all over the country; he even sold socialist tracts and papers in the streets. Outside his own artistic field, however, Morris was not much of an original thinker and he drew heavily on Marx for his political inspiration, though he was never able to get very far with the economic analysis of his master.

His socialism was primarily a fierce emotional protest and an assertion that fraternity and beauty were as vital to life as bread. Though he had a pretty clear view of historical materialism, Morris was content to leave the study of the dialectic and the theory of value to other minds more capable of dealing with them. Socialism, for him, was both necessary and possible, and that was enough to justify all his efforts to achieve it. While Morris learnt the conception of the class-struggle from Marx, he interpreted it to mean that the revolutionary seizure of power was the sole aim of working-class organization. This led him, for a considerable time, into an attitude of outright hostility towards parliamentary action, and towards any kind of reformism. Both, he was sure, served only to divert the proletariat from revolution and to keep the detested system tottering on for a little longer. He drifted towards anarchism in his hope that communism could be established on the morrow of a successful revolt, without any need for a transition period.

As the prospect of immediate revolution faded—and it had never been bright—Morris realized that the tide of events was running in the direction of State socialism, though to the end of his life he remained sceptical of electoral reform. He feared that the socialist movement might sink into the morass of cautious respectability, might become so absorbed in pettifogging details of administration that a system of State-regulated capitalism might be mistaken for the spirit and substance of real socialism, of a society of practical equality. To the last, Morris remained an uncompromising revolutionary, struggling, as he said of himself, "to set the crooked straight". In artistic taste, as in politics, he was one of the great formative influences on modern England. The direct successes of this generous and lovable man were few: his indirect achievements have been varied and immense.

While Morris and Hyndman appeared to be in the political wilderness, their work had repercussions in the very place where they expected least results—the trade unions. The "new unionism" had not only begun to change the outlook of the whole movement on industrial matters; it had also produced a new attitude to political activity. During the slump of the early 'nineties the new unions did not disintegrate like their predecessors which had tried to organize the unskilled workers. Their politics held their members together in much the same way as the vested financial interests had been a source of strength for the craft unions in difficult times. At each annual Trades Union Congress there was a growing minority which demanded that the unions should sponsor their own candidates for Parliament, while local organizations were formed in different parts of the country to support the idea of an independent working-class party. In the middle of the 'eighties the unions had actually set up a Labour Electoral Association which boasted of eleven Members of Parliament, but this group broke up when the Liberal Party undertook to include a number of Labour candidates in its list. For some years there was continuous friction between the sections of the trade union movement which supported the Liberals in return for the nomination of a handful of trade unionists in working-class constituencies, and the socialist organizations which insisted on putting their own men up against the Liberals whenever they thought fit.

The alliance between the Labour representatives in Parliament and the Liberal Party which provided them with a refuge was a further stimulant to those who wanted a separate party which was committed neither to the Marxism of the Social-Democratic Federation nor to the Liberals. At the end of the 'eighties Keir Hardie, the leader of the Ayrshire miners, had started a socialist movement in Scotland which regarded itself as an opponent of the Marxists. By 1893 he was able to call a conference in Bradford to form the Independent Labour Party, which was attended by over a hundred delegates from a variety of bodies.

Though this new party was not all that Hardie desired, it was a step towards a mass working-class party which was neither committed to the revolutionary aims of the Marxists nor dependent upon the charity of the Liberals for its existence. The immediate aim of the I.L.P., which was based upon a vague and moderate socialist programme, was to contest local and national elections. In this it did not meet with much success, though its leaders were perfectly willing to trim their slogans to the electoral wind. It was soon clear that the I.L.P., although it stood much closer to the position of compromise adopted by a majority of the workers than the Marxists, could not get sufficient trade union backing to become the kind of party Hardie wanted to build. He was seeking to form an alliance between the unions, which had the money and the membership to sponsor a large number of Labour candidates, and the socialists, who would provide a virile leadership. In 1899 a motion was passed at the Trades Union Congress instructing its Parliamentary Committee to call a special conference "to devise ways and means for the securing of an increased number of Labour Members in the next Parliament".

This conference met in February 1900 and there was an immediate clash between the representatives of the I.L.P. and those of the Social-Democratic Federation, which had been invited to take part in the discussions. The I.L.P. was more concerned with the formation of a Labour group in Parliament which would be distinct from the Liberals than with the programme of this group, believing that any attempt to foist a socialist policy upon Labour men who were reluctant to make any break at all with the Liberals would wreck the negotiations from the start.

The Marxists, however, asked what point there was in forming a new group if it was not given any definite political instructions. It was obvious, they said, that the group, though nominally independent, would continue to function as little more than an appendage of the Liberals. But the I.L.P. proposal, which was put up as a compromise to offset the challenge of a far less socialist resolution, was carried, and the Labour Representation Committee was set up. In the elections of 1900 the candidates sponsored by the L.R.C., apart from Hardie and Bell, were defeated, though ten "Labour" candidates were elected on the Liberal list. All of them refused to have anything to do with the L.R.C.

When, in the following year, a second conference was

held, it was reported that the affiliated union membership of the L.R.C. had increased only from 375,000 to 469,000, and that of a total of one thousand unions a mere handful had applied for affiliation to the L.R.C. At this conference another attempt by the Marxists in the S.D.F. to tie the new movement down to a definite statement of principle was defeated. It looked as though the Labour Representation Committee was doomed to the same failure as its predecessors, and the delegates from the Social-Democratic Federation, disillusioned and suspicious, withdrew from it.

This defeatism was premature, for the whole position was changed by a new threat to the legal standing of the trade unions. Under the Acts passed in the 'Seventies the union officials had been secured against criminal prosecutions, and it was assumed that, as corporate bodies, they also enjoyed immunity from civil proceedings to recover losses caused to the employers by strikes. In 1901, following a strike in South Wales, the Taff Vale Railway Company took the Amalgamated Society of Railway Servants to the House of Lords and was awarded twenty-three thousand pounds damages. This decision was a major disaster to the trade union movement. As long as it was allowed to stand it was almost impossible for a union to allow its members to strike for fear of being involved in ruinous legal actions. In self-defence the unions had to throw themselves into the struggle to reverse this judgment by legislation.

This crisis saved the Labour Representation Committee. In less than two years its affiliated unions numbered nearly two hundred, with a total membership of one million. These unions introduced a political levy on their members and devoted the greater part of the funds thus raised to the L.R.C. At the elections of 1906 the L.R.C. put up fifty candidates, twenty-nine of whom were returned. For the first time the Liberal-Labour men were in a minority, only fourteen of them being elected. In the same year the L.R.C. was reconstituted as the Labour Party, retaining its form as a federation of trade unions and socialist organizations, with its own party and not a mere group in Parliament. Among the latter was the Fabian Society, which had joined the L.R.C. in 1900, and which was to become the dominant theoretical influence in the new party.

CHAPTER IX

THE FABIANS AND THE LABOUR PARTY

THE Taff Vale judgment forced the trade unions to affiliate to their own distinct Labour Party, but it did not suddenly convert them to socialism. Yet the new party required some sort of distinctive philosophy. It was obviously illogical for it to oppose Liberal candidates at the polls and still accept the traditional doctrines of Liberalism. It was even more illogical to expect that trade union leaders, fresh from the Liberal fold and devoted to constitutional reform, would pay any attention to the handful of Marxists in the Social-Democratic Federation. In the reformist socialism of the Fabian Society the young party found what it needed. The Fabian outlook has ever since dominated the socialist movement in Britain.

Unlike most other socialist organizations, the Fabian Society was never meant to do the work of a political party. From its foundation in 1884 it was intended to be a small propagandist body of intellectuals who, sharing a common desire for social reform, would try to secure the changes they sought through the agency of whatever individuals or organizations they could win, by persuasion or permeation, to their side. It was led from the beginning by some of the most brilliant minds of the time, notably George Bernard Shaw, Beatrice and Sidney Webb.

The tactics adopted by the Fabians were a direct reflection of their attitude to society. Although, until the local Fabian Societies merged themselves with the I.L.P., they did have fairly close contacts with some parts of the working-class movement, they were equally, if not more, ready to concentrate on permeation of the Liberal Party, which seemed the most likely sponsor for their detailed schemes of reorganization for everything from slaughter-houses to railways.

Believing that society developed by a steady progression of small functional and structural changes, rather than by revolutionary leaps, especially where it is ruled by democratic methods, the Fabians naturally regarded every reform that extended the scope of public ownership or control as an instalment of socialism, the socialist commonwealth thus being reached gradually and almost imperceptibly. They rejected, in a somewhat summary fashion, the Marxist analysis of capitalism. Indeed, Edward Pease, the official historian of the Fabian Society, claimed that "its first achievement . . . was to break the spell of Marxism in England". In place of the labour theory of value, which had been the main analytical conception of socialist economics up to that point, the Fabians formulated a different approach to capitalism, based on "economic science as taught by the accredited British professors". According to the theories of John Stuart Mill, who may be regarded as the real parent of the "British" theory of socialism, and of Jevons, on whom the Fabians drew heavily, there were natural laws of supply and demand which automatically ensured that the worker received the wage that was his due, that the capitalist had a reward for the use of his money, and that the community was provided with the goods and services it most required.

This doctrine of marginal utility, as it is known, was an extremely sophisticated justification of private enterprise. Though the Fabians did not accept the conclusions which the defenders of capitalism drew from this analysis, for they advocated the abolition of the capitalist system whose workings it attempted to explain, their own doctrine shows considerable evidence of its influence upon them. They suggested, however, that the origin of the unearned incomes of landlord and employers alike was the rent that they received from their ownership of the means of production and not, as Marx insisted, the surplus-value created by the workers.

It followed from this that private ownership was undesirable and ought slowly to be reformed out of existence. The Fabians did not believe, however, that there was any urgent reason why socialism should replace capitalism. Certainly, on moral and political grounds, they hoped it would. But, basing their analysis on the theories of the foremost capitalist economists, they assumed that society would not necessarily run into disaster even if the arrival of socialism were to be postponed indefinitely.

The attitude of the Fabian Society towards the working-class movement was a logical result of this economic outlook. It presumed that there was a growing identity of interest between the employers and their workers; that living standards would continue to rise and unemployment diminish; and that socialism was the most rational form of social organization which all reasonable men in the community could be persuaded to accept. In view of its failure to capture the Liberal Party by permeation and the evident reluctance of a majority of the employers to assist in their own painless liquidation, the Fabian Society associated itself with the demand for a separate Labour Party and then, having helped in the formation of that party, began to use it as the instrument for achieving the desired reforms.

But this did not mean that the Fabians had been convinced that their effort to secure social change by general consent was futile and that, as the Marxists argued, a socialist system could be established only by a working-class that spurned all collaboration with its exploiters and set out to dispossess them by the seizure of political power in the State that they controlled. On the contrary, the Fabians shared the prevailing view of radical reformers and of the dominant section of the men who formed the Labour Party that there was no clear division between capitalist and socialist society, that the one would step by step be transformed into the other by the process of legislative action. It was the duty of the workers to elect as many representatives as possible to Parliament, and to the municipalities, to assist that process.

By the constitutional methods of democracy the Fabians believed the land and the factories, the gasworks and the railways could be transferred from private ownership to the State. But their view of the State was very different from that of the Marxists. It seemed to them a completely neutral force in society. Its powers and functions, they thought, were at the disposal of any group that commanded a majority in the House of Commons.

It was, in a sense, an enormous version of a Government Department, impersonal and efficient. To ask, as the Marxists asked, what social class controlled the State and shaped its policy, was a meaningless question to the Fabians, who refused to accept the idea that society was divided into opposing classes. They saw the State as the centre of the administrative machine and denied, as far as they considered the matter, that it was also an instrument of class rule and coercion.

They did not, therefore, anticipate any difficulty in using the existing State to accomplish the transition to socialism; it appeared to be a neutral agency which could be used as easily for this as for any other purpose. There was no need to reconstruct it, as the Marxists asserted, to ensure that its structure reflected the new social conditions. Such alterations as were required could be made piecemeal as its powers were gradually extended. After a good many years had passed, it is true, the Fabians began to reconsider their judgment about the nature of the State. But they never discarded their conviction that in a democracy based upon universal suffrage the State was always at the disposal of the majority, or that the machinery of parliamentary democracy was eminently suitable for the establishment of socialism by consent.

The Fabians were primarily concerned with domestic and particular reforms, and in this they were responsible for some considerable achievements. They understood that they were more likely to get the things they wanted done if they concentrated their efforts upon definite and detailed proposals for handing water supplies over to local authorities, or eliminating anomalies from the system of poor relief, than if they dissipated their strength in trying to cover the whole field of international politics.

They consequently took very little notice of foreign affairs. When the Boer War broke out a Fabian manifesto declared that this was an issue "which Socialism cannot solve and does not touch", though Bernard Shaw later published a pamphlet called *Fabianism and the Empire*, in which he justified imperialism on the grounds that an advanced nation had the right to conquer a backward people in the name of efficiency and progress. The Fabian Society reacted similarly to the outbreak of war in 1914, declining to make any statement of policy.

Socialism, in the Fabian sense, thus became a technique of legislative reform within the framework of a capitalist society. The task of the Fabians, as they conceived it, was not to overturn that society but to hasten, by piecemeal modification, its already evident drift towards collectivism. They were not particularly impressed by the Marxist analysis of the tendencies in capitalist development. They thought that Marx had been wrong in almost every prediction he made, and they summarily rejected his argument that capitalism would inevitably run into a series of catastrophic wars and economic crises.

Although the Fabian Society was never a large body—in 1906 it defeated a proposal made by H. G. Wells that it should turn itself into a national organization with a big membership —it succeeded in imposing its views upon an increasingly important section of the Labour Party, and in 1918 its efforts were crowned with success and the party adopted a nominally socialist programme. As early as 1906, however, the secretary of the Labour Party, Ramsay MacDonald, had stated the principles upon which the new party was based in terms which reflected the influence of the Fabians. It must resist any attempt to present it purely as a movement of the workers, MacDonald said, for these principles were not reached "by a process of economic reasoning or of working-class experience". On the contrary, they rested "upon conceptions of right and wrong common to all classes".

This attitude was typical of the Parliamentary Labour Party in the years up to 1914. Its independent political activity was confined to issues about which the trade unions felt strongly and about which the Liberals were reluctant to do anything unless they were pushed; its socialism never went as far as the limits set by the Fabians, the only theorists it possessed. After the Liberal victory in 1906 a new Trades Disputes Act was passed to reverse the Taff Vale judgment; the eight-hour day introduced into the coal mines; old-age pensions, and free meals for school-children provided; and the system of workmen's compensation extended.

But the trade unions began to feel that all these things might have been done, anyway, by the Liberals, without any need for the expense and trouble of maintaining a Labour group in Parliament. Their interest in the latter was obviously waning when yet another attack was made upon their legal rights. In 1909 the House of Lords decided in the Osborne case that it was illegal for trade unions to devote any of their funds to political purposes. Indeed, this judgment raised doubts about the legality of other activities of the trade unions, about their association in trades councils, and even in the Trades Union Congress. The unions once more rallied behind their own party to work for legislation which would remove the serious restrictions placed upon their activity by the Osborne judgment.

There was, however, a growing section of the trade union movement which wanted nothing to do with politics as practised by the Labour representatives in Parliament. Ten years before it had been the most radical workers who had demanded the formation of their own party and the moderate union leaders who had insisted that the movement should confine itself to industrial matters. These positions were now reversed. While their leaders were praising the virtues of legislative reform, the militant workers were preparing for direct industrial action on a large scale. It was by no means the unskilled workers only who were ready for a head-on conflict with the employers. In fact, the very unions who had previously preferred arbitration and the automatic adjustment of wages by a system of sliding scales, especially the miners, were willing to fight both their employers and their union leaders, taking the lead in the series of strikes that started about 1908. One of the main reasons for this change of front was the tendency of real wages to fall.

Up to the end of the nineteenth century, however money wages had fluctuated, there was a general and fairly steady rise in real wages due to the decline of commodity prices. In the first decade of the present century real wages were dropping again, and the workers realized that they could maintain their position only by considerable increases in money wages. They wanted these advances quickly, and were not prepared to wait for the lengthy processes of arbitration or accept the operation of old agreements which often provided for a reduction of wages at the very moment the workers concerned desired them to go up.

This new temper was responsible for many great strikes, dislocating the transport of a number of cities, the railways all over the country and coal production, to say nothing of scores of less spectacular disputes that accompanied them. In 1904 less than two million working days were lost in strikes; in 1912 the total was over forty million. A "Triple Alliance" was formed by the transport workers, the railwaymen and the miners with the object of organizing a general strike for their demands. Yet the rising curve of industrial unrest was almost entirely dissociated from the Parliamentary Labour Party, in which many of the strike leaders had little faith or interest, since they regarded all parliamentary politics as a diversion from the real struggle of the working-class.

In this struggle they believed the picket-lines rather than the polling-booths to be the scene of the fight against capitalism and the employers. Under the influence of French syndicalism (which is discussed below), and the industrial unionism in the United States, the extreme Left had abandoned all hope of salvation through constitutional reform and had turned to direct industrial action as the one effective means by which the workers could win control of industry. They despised the State socialism of the Fabians; they did not want mere nationalization, as the famous pamphlet *The Miners' Next Step* explained. Strike action alone would push wages so high that it would be unprofitable for the employers to carry on. The workers themselves would then take over and operate the mines and the factories.

Accompanying this syndicalist agitation, though on a more sophisticated plane, was the propaganda of the Guild socialists. Their policy was as much a reaction from Fabianism on the intellectual level as syndicalism was from the role played by the Labour representatives in Parliament and the ideas of industrial harmony still supported by a part of the trade union leadership.

Some of the Guild socialists, such as G. D. H. Cole, for instance, had actually broken away from the Fabian Society. They did not believe, as the syndicalists believed, that the State and political action could be disregarded completely, at least for some time. Neither did they share the Fabians' conviction that the State was a neutral machine of administration and not the instrument through which a particular social class dominated the rest of society in its own interests. They disliked the State precisely as a machine of administration and desired to limit rather than increase its powers to direct production, distribution and people. The transformation of England into a socialist commonwealth, they thought, was a matter of changing its economic structure, without any need for the workers first to seize power.

Consequently, like the followers of Owen and Proudhon, who had been equally sceptical of the value of political methods, they sought to begin the transition to socialism by creating, within society as they found it, the kind of economic organization they desired. Similarly, they concentrated upon drafting elaborate projects for the actual operation of the industries they proposed to socialize.

The Guild socialist movement sprang from a number of sources. Its leaders were greatly influenced by the views of William Morris and John Ruskin, both of whom had bitterly attacked the way in which capitalism had produced a cult of the machine at the expense of the individual's sense of craftsmanship and beauty. Seeking, as Morris had sought, to restore the dignity of labour, they turned for inspiration to the medieval self-governing guilds, in which they believed that men had been offered an outlet for their creative instincts. They wished to reverse the whole scale of moral and aesthetic standards which capitalism had imposed. The wage system, for the Guild socialists, was spiritually and economically intolerable, for it both corrupted the personality of the worker and exploited him. Service to the community, they said, should be the only criterion of production; the idea of profit should be eliminated.

This was to be accomplished by setting up a number of National Guilds, each of which would be responsible for the operation of a particular industry. These Guilds would be organized nationally in a Guilds Congress which would have the same sort of control over the economic activity of the country as Parliament had over its political and foreign affairs. The Guilds would be self-governing, thus giving the worker an adequate chance to participate in the control of the industry in which he worked, and as a result an opportunity for the proper expression of his personality. Industries socialized in this fashion would be able to offer far better standards of payment —apart from the more intangible rewards—since the only interests that had to be considered would be those of the producers and consumers who formed the community. There would be no idle rich or unearned incomes under Guild socialism.

In all this the trade unions were cast in a leading role. Since the processes of social change were economic rather than political, the Guild socialists considered, the unions—and these were to be industrial unions—were the most suitable instruments for creating the desired National Guilds. They could not do this, however, unless they realized that their functions could not be confined to securing mere improvements in wages and working conditions; they had to aim higher than that, endeavouring to abolish the system of wage labour entirely, and to take an increasing share in controlling the supply of labour, its reward and its part in the management of industry.

In general, the philosophy of the Guild socialists was far more radical and coherent than that of the Fabians. They were not content merely to wait until the slow accumulation of reforms carried England into a bureaucratic State socialism; they wished to undertake the transition as quickly as possible, even if it involved an extensive recasting of existing institutions.

In the new society there would be no single centre of authority able to direct every social activity without challenge. The Guild socialists wanted as much decentralization of administration as of industrial management and control. Since they saw the State as but the largest of a whole series of bodies in which men came together for a common purpose—such as the churches, trade unions, political parties, and even recreational organizations, each of which contributed an indispensable element to the life of its members—they sought to give each of these bodies the fullest freedom to control its own specific activities as was compatible with any kind of order and unity within society.

Naturally, in their plan of things, they allowed the State to retain some of its powers, provided that these did not restrict unnecessarily the liberty of all the other associations, but they never accepted the view that the State, as such, had an overriding claim upon the services of its subjects, irrespective of their own feelings.

Guild socialism, however, did not become a mass movement, and though it survived throughout the war of 1914-18—the National Guilds League was actually formed in 1915 after nearly ten years of propaganda by Orage, Penty and S. G. Hobson, who, with Cole, were the most prominent Guild socialists—it dwindled rapidly in the post-war years as the growing strength of the Parliamentary Labour Party enhanced the prospect of a Labour Government along the lines desired by the Fabians, and as the Left wing of the Guild socialists joined the Communists.

Nevertheless, it did a good deal to revive controversy and to stimulate theoretical discussion about the *kind* of socialism which was practicable and desirable in England. Its appearance was, above all, a sign that the working-class movement in England was unable to get much further by repeating the old slogans and muddling on from one crisis to the next without any clear idea of where it eventually wanted to go. So far, it has not gone in the direction suggested by the Guild socialists, but their work did at least draw attention to the danger of regarding the transition to socialism as merely a matter of administrative reorganization in the interests of efficiency. Like Morris, the Guild Socialists wanted a social regeneration.

CHAPTER X

GERMAN SOCIAL-DEMOCRACY

IN the thirty years after 1870 the German socialist movement became the most powerful in Europe. Until the 'seventies, as we have already seen, it was split into rival sections, one under the leadership of Schweitzer, who had succeeded Lassalle, and the other led by Wilhelm Liebknecht and August Bebel, who were supporters of Marx and of the First International. In the elections of 1871 the two groups polled over a hundred thousand votes between them. This aggregate vote rose to 340,000 in January, 1874, the Lassallians securing three seats in the Reichstag and the Eisenach fraction winning six.

These electoral successes soon attracted the attention of the Reich Government, and both parties were faced with a campaign of persecution. In this difficult period they began to discover how much they had in common. Their representatives in the Reichstag had fought the elections on similar programmes and worked together for the same demands and against the same enemies. The legal existence of both parties was threatened by judgments secured by Tessendorff, the public prosecutor. The main obstacles to unity, in fact, were the memory of old quarrels and some theoretical differences whose importance did not seem to be very great compared with the practical difficulties confronting the two sections. In October 1874 negotiations for their fusion began.

For a time Liebknecht kept these negotiations secret from Marx and Engels in London. He did not attach so much weight as they did to theoretical matters, and he was perfectly willing to make very considerable concessions to the Lassallians in order to get them into the united party as quickly as possible. He knew that Marx was opposed to fusion for fear that the new party might fall into the hands of the numerically stronger Lassallians. Thus when Marx and Engels finally saw the draft programme upon which the two parties had agreed, it was too late for them to do anything. Though they protested in the strongest terms to both Liebknecht and Bebel, they secured nothing more than a few trifling alterations in the text. The programme was adopted by the unity congress that met at Gotha in 1875.

Marx and Engels denounced the programme as an intolerable compromise, but their criticisms were ignored in Germany. None of their supporters realized that the two exiles in London were not simply splitting hairs but raising extremely serious theoretical issues. To the men on the spot, who were chiefly interested in the practical benefits that would result from unity, it did not seem to matter much if the paper programme had to be watered down to meet the demands of the Lassallians. They did not understand that there was a major difference of principle between the views of Marx and those to which the programme committed the movement. The *Gotha Programme* paid no attention to trade unions; it denied the possibility of effective international working-class activity; and it took over the Lassallian conception of the State as a neutral instrument of government which could be directed, once the workers had an electoral majority, to socialist purposes. Marx, on the contrary, believed that if the movement accepted this reformist outlook uncritically, the workers would be diverted from their real task, which was to overthrow capitalism and the State associated with it.

But his critique made no impression on the leaders of the new party. It was clear that those who professed to be Marxists shared in the prevailing theoretical confusion. In spite of their respect for Marx and Engels, few of them had any idea of Marxism as a coherent and comprehensive philosophy. When, however, numbers of them began to turn to the wordy and pretentious arguments of a Berlin professor called Dühring, Engels decided that it was time he set down a clear statement of the principles of socialism for which he and Marx stood. He did not know that his polemical book *Anti-Dühring* was, in the long run, to play a decisive part in winning the socialist movement in Europe for Marxism. Yet this book stated in a lucid fashion just how Marx and Engels interpreted both the course of history and the events of their own day. It not only won over the most brilliant young socialists to Marxism, but the reprint of the political chapters, *Socialism, Utopian and Scientific*, was circulated almost as widely as the *Communist Manifesto*, with which it must rank in influence. It took some years for this work to accomplish the conversion of the German and other socialist movements, but there is little doubt that its publication marks the point at which Marxism began to establish its supremacy over other socialist doctrines.

Despite the theoretical dissensions inside the party, it made rapid headway. In the elections of 1877 it polled more than 500,000 votes and sent twelve representatives to the Reichstag. But its increasing strength brought it in conflict with the authorities, who determined to check its progress before the party was properly consolidated. Two unsuccessful attempts on the life of the Emperor in 1878 provided a suitable excuse for repressive legislation, although the party was free from all responsibility in both cases.

The Anti-Socialist Laws, which were passed at the instigation of Bismarck, almost broke up the party. Some of its leaders were exiled; it could neither hold public meetings nor publish newspapers. The only socialists who could speak with any freedom were the dozen members in the Reichstag. But a majority of these held that the only way to hold the movement together was to abandon the radical principles on which it was based and to co-operate with the progressive bourgeois parties. The minority, which included Bebel and Liebknecht, struggled hard to act as the spokesman of the persecuted revolutionary workers, who had no other legal means of expression.

In this period of illegality it was obviously necessary for the party machinery to be held together from abroad. It therefore fell to the exiles to organize the congresses of the party and to publish its paper, the *Social-Democrat*, thousands of copies of which were smuggled into Germany, first from Zurich and later from London. For most of this time the editor of the paper was Eduard Bernstein, who afterwards became the leading critic of Marxism inside the party.

While Bismarck had no hesitation about repressing the socialists, he was intelligent enough to realize that he could not destroy their influence unless the workers were compensated for the loss of liberty by social reforms. In 1882 he put forward legislation providing accident and sickness insurance. Old-age pensions followed. Bismarck was ready, as he had admitted in introducing the Anti-Socialist Laws, to accept a good deal of what had once been demanded by Lassalle, such as the nationalization of transport, the equalization of wealth through taxation, and the stabilization of employment through State action.

Nevertheless, for all Bismarck could do, the socialists gained ground. In 1884 they polled 549,000; in 1887, 763,000. By 1890, in spite of the laws restricting their activity, they had become the largest single party in the Reich, securing 1,427,000 votes. It was clearly impossible to hold them in check by persecution, and the Anti-Socialist Laws were abandoned. The party then had to take stock of its position, after more than ten years, in which it had been unable to meet openly or provide for free consultation between the leaders and the rank-and-file. It was soon clear that the Marxists now dominated the party; at Erfurt in 1891 the party congress accepted their draft of a new programme to replace the old one which had been adopted at Gotha.

Though this programme said nothing about historical materialism or the theory of surplus value, it included the main principles on which Marx had insisted that any effective working-class party should be based. It recognized that the struggle of the workers against capitalism could not be confined to politics, as Lassalle had sought to do, or to economic reorganization, as Proudhon believed, but had to be carried on in both spheres at the same time. It insisted that it was the task of the Social-Democratic Party to lead this struggle and to give the workers a consciousness of their mission to emancipate the whole of society by converting private property into social property and capitalist into socialist production. It declared, finally, that the class-struggle was not limited to the boundaries of a single nation, since all workers had common interests and that the party was, therefore, internationalist.

The programme then outlined the immediate demands of the party, such as the separation of Church and State, free education, medical services and legal facilities, progressive taxation, protective labour legislation, unrestricted rights of speech and assembly, and the full legal recognition of trade union organizations. After thirty years of intensive effort it seemed that the Marxists at last had the biggest working-class party in the world marching squarely behind them.

This Marxist victory, however, did not mean that the revolutionary wing of the party, which was convinced that peaceful reform alone would never break the strength of the capitalist system, had decisively routed the moderates, who sought to win power by constitutional methods. On the contrary, the rise of the Social-Democratic Party to a leading place in German politics only sharpened the conflict between the two sections. The main difference produced by the nominal conversion of the party to Marxist doctrine was that both wings of the party felt obliged to couch their arguments in Marxist terms, justifying their position by detailed and elaborate reference to the texts of the Marxist classics. Once the party had won a considerable number of seats in the Reichstag, many of its candidates receiving almost as much support from middle-class voters as from the workers, it had to decide whether it should accept its new role as a successful and comparatively respectable parliamentary body, or whether it should run the risk of further repression and of losing many of its more cautious supporters by holding to the spirit as well as the letter of Marxism. In the end the decision went in favour of the moderates, but the controversy was not easily settled.

The split between the two groups was quite obvious by the end of the 'nineties. For some time the socialists in Southern Germany, where industry was not so highly developed and political institutions were rather more democratic than in Prussia, had been criticizing the party leadership for interpreting Marxism too literally. The party, they said, could only get the backing of the rural population if it stopped dogmatizing about the inherent tendencies of capitalist society, and set about winning some immediate practical reforms.

This discontent, moreover, was not limited to one area. All through the party organization there was a growing number of members who dismissed the traditional propositions of Marxism as inadequate and demanded that the party should revise the theoretical assumptions on which it was based. The bank clerk, Eduard Bernstein, who had become a party functionary and who had edited the illegal edition of the party organ from Zurich, became the chief spokesman of this group of "revisionists", as they were called.

Bernstein left Germany in the year that the Anti-Socialist Laws were passed, spending the next twenty-two years in Switzerland and England before he returned home in 1900. For a time he had been a close associate of Engels and he was regarded as one of the most brilliant of the younger Marxists. But, as the years went on, he became more and more convinced that much of the Marxist analysis of capitalism was either wrong or obsolete. He was also an intimate friend of some of the leaders of the Fabian Society, and he was considerably influenced by their rejection of Marx and their belief in the gradual evolution of society towards a system of State socialism. He was, in fact, destined to play much the same role in Germany as they had in the British Labour Movement.

Eduard Bernstein began his attack upon the orthodox Marxists in a series of articles written for the party's theoretical paper, *Neue Zeit*, following these up with a long letter to a party conference that met in Stuttgart in 1898, and with his book, *Evolutionary Socialism*, which appeared in 1899. Marx was wrong, Bernstein declared, in believing that the collapse of the capitalist system was imminent. Nor was he right in predicting that the gulf between the various classes in society would become wider and the class-struggle more bitter as the ownership of the means of production became concentrated in the hands of fewer and fewer people.

On the contrary, the development of the joint-stock company, in which ownership was dispersed among many thousands of shareholders, meant that there was "an increasing number of capitalists of all degrees". The middle-class was not disappearing but was becoming larger and more important. The advance of political democracy, the emergence of a State which was willing to recognize trade unions, to limit the exploitation of the worker by protective legislation, and to introduce a national system of social welfare and insurance, diminished both the need and the opportunity for the catastrophic change which Marx had anticipated.

There was, Bernstein insisted, no final aim of socialism:

socialists should not display an excessive interest in some future society whose nature was unpredictable. "The movement," he said, in a famous phrase, "is everything." The party should concentrate its efforts on securing, one by one, the definite and limited reforms which, in aggregate, would gradually transfer control of society from a "commercial land-holding oligarchy to a real democracy". The labour theory of value, Bernstein argued, was little more than an abstract image. It was no use as a means of investigating the actual working of a capitalist economy. Similarly, Marx had produced a muddled and inadequate explanation of the periodic economic crises.

There was no evidence that, owing to the inability of capitalism to overcome its internal contradictions, these crises would become increasingly violent, culminating in a general collapse. Indeed, Bernstein believed that the enormous expansion of the wealth and trade of the main industrial countries, the elasticity of their credit system and the development of trusts and combines, had made capitalism more stable and that further great economic depressions were improbable. Socialists, consequently, had to look rather to the steady transformation of society by democratic methods than to the revolutionary tactics proposed by Marx in the days when the workers had no political rights and were confronted with a hostile State, dominated by the employers who exploited them. For the socialist movement was the heir to liberalism, with its regard for personal liberty, and it could not accept the thesis that the flexible liberal institutions of modern society should be overthrown and replaced by a dictatorship of the proletariat. That, Bernstein said, "belongs to a lower civilization, and apart from the expediency and practicability of the thing, it is only to be looked upon as a reversion".

Thus, for Bernstein as for the Fabians, the State was not a class organization. It was a partnership in which the workers had secured a considerable stake. They would accomplish all they desired through the intelligent use of their votes, without any real resistance from the capitalists, for "the rights of the propertied minority have ceased to be a serious obstacle to social progress".

With these arguments, elaborated continually throughout the next ten years, Bernstein provoked the most intense theoretical controversy, not only in the ranks of the Social-Democratic Party, but also among the socialist movements in other countries where Marxism had any influence. In this period, everything that Marx and Engels had either said or written was subjected to the closest scrutiny to prove that it was, or was not, applicable to the more highly developed capitalist structure with which socialists had to reckon. It was, in fact, a dispute of critical importance in the history of socialism. (And for us, today. For the argument about the tactics of a minority movement at the end of the nineteenth century has become a quarrel between States, now that both communists and moderate socialists have become governments in a number of countries. At bottom, the same issues divide Russia and the West as once divided the Labour movement into warring factions.) Was the movement in Europe to declare, as it had in England, that the revolutionary road to power was inappropriate in a democracy, that the capitalists would abdicate without a violent struggle, and that, in due course, by the steady accumulation of reforms, the socialist commonwealth would be achieved? Or was it to decide that the capitalist system could not afford concessions indefinitely, that it could not avoid relapsing into disastrous economic crises and, ultimately, into imperialist wars? If it accepted the first policy, it would certainly regard the revolutionary Marxists as greater enemies of progress than the capitalists. If, however, it heeded the warnings of the Left, it would prepare for a long and bitter fight for power, in which there would be no quarter from either side.

For the Left believed that if the advance of socialism within a capitalist democracy challenged the property rights of the ruling-class on a large scale, that class would be more ready to abolish the hard-won democratic rights of the workers than to give up its own wealth and privileges. Should the working-class pin its faith entirely on legal action and the possibility of change by general consent, it would find itself leaderless and impotent at the very moment when war or economic crisis offered it the opportunity of winning power. By fostering the illusion that capitalism had changed its whole nature, especially since the development of the trusts, Bernstein and his associates, the Marxists said, were leading the movement to disaster.

But the Marxists themselves were by no means united. A few of them maintained an uncompromisingly revolutionary attitude and, as in the case of Rosa Luxemburg and the younger Liebknecht, later became the founders of the Spartacist League, the forerunner of the German Communist Party. Most of them followed the lead of Karl Kautsky, one of the most eminent Marxist theoreticians, who began as a strong opponent of Bernstein and later, in his hostility to communism, drifted into the company of the "revisionists".

Thus, in spite of its nominal commitment to Marxism, the Social-Democratic Party was split into warring factions. The Right wing of the party was quite open in its support for German imperialism, justifying it on much the same grounds as Shaw had endorsed the British war against the Boers and indulging at times in the most fervid eulogies of their country's civilizing mission. The Centre had become so obsessed with practical reforms and philosophical abstractions that it had lost any realistic perspective of current developments, and almost to the outbreak of war in 1914 was asserting that there was no question of conflict because leading statesmen had assured the world that they desired peace. Though copious references were still made to Marx and to the traditions of the party, both these sections had become so involved in the politics of the German Empire that they had almost no idea at all where the Reich was heading.

Every time the radical elements in the party demanded that it should remember the traditional socialist opposition to militarism or should prepare itself for the impending war, they were denounced by both Right and Centre as extremists who were imperilling the striking progress the party had already made towards socialism. It was true that it was still the largest socialist movement in the world, with a vast organization, a large number of newspapers and an impressive vote at elections. But it was a movement whose internal weaknesses were to be tragically exposed in the course of the war of 1914–18, and in the immediate post-war years.

In the conflict between the moderates and the revolution-aries the moderates had won, for very much the same reason as the Labour Party in England had passed under the leadership of the Fabians instead of the Social-Democratic Federation. German capitalism, like its English counterpart, passed through a period of expansion and prosperity, though the period was shorter and the prosperity not so great. It is characteristic of such periods that the socialist movement loses its militancy and endeavours to find a basis of compromise with the existing system.

Naturally, there were important differences between the Labour Party and the German Social-Democrats, not the least of which was the way in which the latter continued to repeat many of the traditional Marxist phrases long after they had ceased to have any relation with the practical policy of the Social-Democratic leaders. But Marxism was unimportant in England. The Labour movement inherited the tradition of radicalism from Bentham and J. S. Mill. Thus the Fabians found the ground already tilled for them when they set out to control the Labour Party. In Germany, however, as in a number of other countries in Europe, there was no other consistent socialist philosophy which had survived the impact of Marxism. Thus those who were really liberal reformers had to come forward as revisors of Marxism and not as its opponents. This paradox was one of the main reasons (the strength of nationalism was another) for the confusion that prevailed in the German Party at the approach and outbreak of the war in 1914.

CHAPTER XI

THE FRENCH LABOUR MOVEMENT

THE violent suppression of the Paris Commune in 1871 broke up the French working-class movement. Many of its leaders were shot in the streets of Paris, imprisoned or driven into exile. In the terror which followed the revolutionary outbreak it was virtually impossible to keep alive either the trade unions or socialist organizations. But the movement made a much quicker recovery from this setback than it had from the defeat of June 1848. Within a few years trade union activity began to revive again.

At first this took place under the leadership of the journalist Barbaret, who believed that trade unions would help to establish industrial peace, would act as educational centres and employment exchanges, and would eventually establish co-operative workshops as a means of eliminating extremes of wealth. By 1876 a large number of these unions had been organized—they were able to capitalize the support given by the French workers to the Proudhonist doctrine of consumers' and producers' co-operatives—and a central congress, attended by over four hundred delegates, was held in Paris. Barbaret must have been well satisfied with his efforts, for this congress went on record against strikes and affirmed the necessity of industrial harmony, refusing to take any notice of the handful of socialists who were present.

Nevertheless, Barbaret's success was comparatively short-lived. A nucleus of socialists—most of them old members of the International—had managed to survive through the difficult period after the Commune. In 1877 they were joined by Jules Guesde, who had returned from exile in Switzerland, where he had been closely associated with the Marxist group. Guesde founded a new weekly paper, *L'Egalité*, which from the start advocated the formation of a proletarian party aiming at the seizure of power and the creation of a socialist society.

Thanks to the agitation carried on by Guesde and his associates, and to the failure of the Proudhonist movement to do anything very much to improve the condition of the workers, the idea of a socialist party began to find increasing support. By the time the third congress of syndicates met at Marseilles in 1879 the socialists were in a majority. Guesde had been sent to prison in the previous year for attempting to hold an international conference of workers in Paris, and this, a resolution passed at Marseilles declared, had shown that "the working-class had no longer to expect its salvation from anybody except itself". It should, therefore, form its own political party and struggle for the collective ownership of the land, the factories and the utility services.

Once the enthusiasts for co-operation and conciliation had been routed, however, the socialists began to differ among themselves. First, there was an anarchist wing which denied that there was anything to be gained from parliamentary politics—which it denounced as leading to corruption, compromise and absurdity—and insisted that only a violent and conclusive insurrection could effectively abolish the twin tyrannies of capitalism and the State. All other forms of socialist activity, the anarchists declared, merely dissipated the revolutionary ardour of the workers. Though it exercised more indirect than direct influence, anarchism was sufficiently similar to the doctrines of Proudhon, on which a whole generation of French workers had been brought up, for it to secure a response among that section of the working-class which still had no faith in normal political measures. In 1883, for instance, after there had been a series of disturbances in mining areas, sixty-six anarchists were put on trial. One of them was Prince Peter Kropotkin, the Russian exile who played a prominent part in the anarchist movement for more than forty years, writing some of its finest historical and philosophical studies.

Apart from the anarchists, there were two other important groups which were divided more or less along the same lines as socialists in other countries. At the congress held in St. Etienne in 1882 the revolutionaries led by Jules Guesde had broken with the reformist wing, headed by Paul Brousse, the first section forming the French Workers' Party and the second adopting the name of the French Socialist Workers' Party.

Guesde had very little belief in the value of reforms. As long as capitalism lasted there was no guarantee that reforms were permanent or that they would not be withdrawn when it suited the ruling-class. Socialists should contest national and local elections because they offered an admirable opportunity for propaganda, not merely to win seats. As the constitution of the party declared, their role was to act as "a kind of recruiting and instructing sergeant", preparing the masses for the seizure of political power in the inevitable crisis.

The Broussists, on the contrary, took much the same line as the Fabians in England and Bernstein in Germany. They believed that it was necessary to concentrate on electoral activity. Their representatives in the municipal or departmental councils, or in the Chamber of Deputies, were to secure the immediate reforms desired by the party by gaining the co-operation of other groups, either by persuasion or permeation. Unlike the revolutionary Marxists, who possessed a strongly-disciplined organization, the reformists gave a good deal of latitude to their local sections and were prepared to admit all manner of persons to their party, provided that they subscribed to the most elementary socialist principles. This, however, did not prevent internal dissensions, and in 1890 a group of members, led by Allemane, broke away to form yet another party on the ground that the Broussists had paid too little attention to socialist agitation and too much to catching votes.

In addition to these four sections of the working-class movement there were two others which exercised some influence. The first—the Central Revolutionary Committee—consisted of former associates and supporters of the veteran conspirator August Blanqui. This group survived until 1904, in one form or another, but its younger members were gradually won over by the Marxists, and the old men, most of whom could not escape from the slogans which had carried them to the barricades in 1848 and 1871, lost touch with the changing feeling in the working-class movement. The second body, which emerged from a discussion circle in much the same way as the Fabian Society, was formed by a number of independent socialists who had become disillusioned with radicalism and turned to drafting schemes of social reform which, they hoped, would be widely endorsed. Some of these men, such as Millerand and Jean Jaurès, later played a prominent part in French politics.

The confusion created by the activity of so many organizations, each claiming that it alone had the insight or ability to lead the French workers, was naturally reflected in the syndicates, whose work was seriously hampered by factional disputes and by the existence of rivals in the same industry or district which owed allegiance to different parties. But as French industry and commerce developed, and the employers maintained their hostility towards all the unions, it became increasingly urgent to form a national federation of syndicates which could unite the workers in the industrial struggles. Though this federation was, in fact, set up at a congress in Lyons in 1886, it soon came under the leadership of the Marxists in the French Workers' Party. When this happened there was no hope of unity, for the other socialist groups refused to participate in the Federation once it had passed under Marxist control. They turned, therefore, to the creation of a parallel body, based on the labour exchanges (*Bourses du Travail*), which, legalized by the law of 1884, were springing up all over France.

Although these exchanges were founded with official assistance, they rapidly became much more than offices where workers could be hired. They acted as centres for local trade union activity, for meetings and for educational classes. Before long this new Federation of Labour Exchanges was dominated by the Allemanists, who, in breaking away from the moderate Socialist Workers' Party, had taken with them some of the most able leaders of the syndicates.

The rival federations were scarcely launched when the old anarchist idea of a general strike began to gain support among the French workers. There were good reasons for this. The possibility of successful revolt in the traditional fashion, of which the anarchists and some of the Blanquists still dreamed, no longer seemed realistic. The prospect of victory through a long political struggle, as envisaged by the socialists, appeared distant and remote. The general strike was thus the sole weapon which the workers could use to emancipate themselves from capitalist exploitation.

In 1888 the Federation of Syndicates endorsed this view; three years later it was taken up by the Allemanists. The remnant of the Blanquists discovered that it fitted perfectly well into their programme. Only the Marxists objected to it. It was childish to imagine, they argued, that a peaceful general strike was possible. Revolutions could not be carried through under a pretence of legality. Even if the workers were willing to abstain from the use of force, there was no sign that the ruling-class would hesitate to suppress a movement which threatened to dispossess it. In any case, the interruption of vital services would bring starvation to the workers long before their employers went hungry. To undertake such an ambitious venture with any chance of success the workers would require to be so well organized and disciplined that they would have already reached the point where they could capture political power.

The Marxist refusal to accept the general strike led to an early breach between them and most of the syndicates. They were unable to stop the passage of a resolution favouring the strike at a conference of the Federation of Syndicates in 1892, and withdrew from it. From this date the Federation—which was changed into the General Confederation of Labour (the C.G.T.) in 1895—declared its independence of all political parties and its support for an early general strike.

For the next few years the policies of the C.G.T. and the Federation of Labour Exchanges ran on converging courses, and in 1903 a united C.G.T. was formed which included them both. By this time, thanks partly to the efforts of Fernand Pelloutier, who was secretary of the Federation of Labour Exchanges until his death in 1901, there was widespread support for syndicalism, as the doctrine of revolution by direct industrial action alone was called.

The syndicalists had moved quite a long way in the direction of anarchism. They had discarded their earlier dislike of violence; they had even gone so far as to endorse sabotage; and they were convinced that the success of a general strike depended less on the resources and discipline of the workers than on the audacious leadership of a purposeful minority. They had also won over a substantial number of socialists who had become disillusioned with the policy of reform and class collaboration pursued by their leaders.

The drift towards syndicalism received a powerful impetus from the Millerand affair. In June 1899 Millerand agreed to enter the Radical Government of Waldeck-Rousseau, which was engaged in a struggle with the monarchist and clerical reaction—personified in the famous Dreyfus case—as Minister of Commerce and Industry. One of his colleagues was the notorious General Gallifet, who had been responsible for the slaughter of thousands of the Communards in 1871. The socialists, at this time, had more than fifty seats in the Chamber of Deputies. An important section, consisting for the most part of the moderate independent socialists and the Broussists, supported Millerand. Jean Jaurès even formulated a new theory for the occasion, arguing that capitalist society had entered a period of transition, in which the proletariat and the bourgeoisie could share power, and that the French socialists would thus be taking the logical course if they endorsed Millerand's decision to accept office.

But this thesis, which raised in an acute form the whole question of the socialist attitude towards reforms and parliamentary politics, was at once contested by the Marxists and the Blanquists, who, unfortunately for them, had no practical alternative to offer. Though the Marxists carried the dispute provoked by the "treachery" of Millerand—and, later, of other socialists—into the international movement, in France at least they were themselves splitting into a reformist wing, which became preoccupied with electoral activity, and a revolutionary wing which drifted towards the syndicalists. The latter, in fact, crying a plague on all schools of socialism, were able to capitalize the resentment and impatience of workers who saw in the Millerand affair a final proof of the futility of dabbling in bourgeois politics.

The syndicalists accepted the Marxist doctrine that society was divided into two warring classes and that the workers were led inevitably to seek the destruction of the capitalist economy. They believed, however, that the syndicate, which united the workers on the basis of their common economic interests, was a far more stable unit of organization than political parties, which, by making a political idea the sole link between men of different social origins and occupations, were liable to be disunited and ephemeral. The syndicate should be an industrial, rather than a craft, union, for this would strengthen the solidarity of the workers and assist in their mobilization for strike action. The general strike, the instrument of social revolution, could not be called until the workers had been prepared for it in a series of strikes, in particular factories, in districts and in whole industries. These strikes would widen the gulf between the employers and the men by revealing the fundamental antagonism that existed between them and at the same time they would teach the workers valuable lessons in tactics and organization.

Since the State was only the means through which the capitalist class exercised its authority—and here again the syndicalists took over a Marxist, or equally an anarchist, argument and adapted it to their own purposes—it should be treated in the same fashion. Such concessions as were necessary should be won by direct action, by street demonstrations. The syndicates should accept only those reforms which were won by force; all the rest were merely attempts to buy them off and should, therefore, be repudiated as liable to blunt the revolutionary temper of the workers.

Similarly, nationalism and militarism served to divide the working-class from its comrades in other lands who were engaged in the same struggle to emancipate themselves. The syndicalists were consequently pledged to oppose all preparations for war and the "patriotic" propaganda that accompanied them. When the general strike was ultimately successful, all private property and class distinctions would be swept away, and the syndicates would then undertake the direction of production and distribution. While such services as the railways would be controlled by the C.G.T. as the most suitable national co-ordinating body, local economic activity would be regulated by the appropriate Labour Exchange, representing all the syndicates in the district. Thus, for the first time, the workers would be drawn into the management of the enterprises in which they were employed. There would be no need for a political State once the necessity for a centralized authority and a means of class oppression had disappeared; such social discipline as would be required in a free and co-operative society would be exercised by the workers themselves.

The syndicalists never went much beyond this in their speculation about the future. They were averse to detailed plans, holding that their task was to change the system and leave the problem of what institutions were to replace it to those who actually had to create them. There was, however, one common point in their philosophy. They regarded majority rule as an illusion. Effective decisions, they said, could be taken only by an organized minority. If it had to submit its aims for the endorsement of the majority, it could not function efficiently. If the majority agreed, the vote was superfluous. If it disagreed, it was obstructing progress.

This principle applied to the work of the syndicates, which, under capitalism, could never hope to rally the entire working-class. They had, therefore, to act as a disinterested leadership and to accomplish, in the best interests of the whole of their class, the overthrow of the employers. The revolution could not wait until everyone realized that it was both desirable and necessary.

Apart from the syndicalists who were active leaders of the labour movement, there was also a small group of intellectuals which sought to construct a more sophisticated doctrine on the basis of the syndical agitation. Of these the most famous was Georges Sorel, who never had much direct influence on the French workers. Sorel insisted that the idea of a general strike was of great value in training and educating the workers for the destruction of capitalism. But it did not matter at all whether this strike ever occurred: it served as a myth to keep up the spirit of the workers in adversity, just as the myth of eternal life had sustained Christianity. Every great social movement, said Sorel, had its myth which served to concentrate its aspirations to the point of action. As long as the workers kept before them the millenial vision of the general strike, their enthusiasm for the fight against capitalism would be kept at fever pitch. This argument was accompanied by a good deal of abstract and mystical moralizing.

Some of Sorel's doctrine, in a crude form, did indeed filter through to the syndicalist rank-and-file, but he himself became more and more reactionary. When, many years later, Mussolini came to set down the rambling and obscure remarks that formed the political testament of Italian fascism, he approvingly incorporated much that he had learnt from Sorel. It was the catastrophic aspect of syndicalism that attracted Sorel. Men, he was convinced, did not become free by changing their environment so much as by their dedication to an heroic cause. They fulfilled themselves only when they substituted moral and physical violence for the placid observance of social conventions.

While the syndicalists were concentrating on their industrial guerilla warfare against capitalism, the various socialist groups were gradually drawing more closely together. In 1905, thanks in part to the intervention of their comrades abroad and in part to the efforts made by Jaurès to unite them, they formed the United Socialist Party. In the next year it polled nearly 900,000 votes and returned fifty-one deputies. Within eight years it had increased its vote to 1,400,000 and the number of its representatives in the Chamber to 103. Some attempt was made to secure the affiliation of the C.G.T., but the syndicates insisted on remaining free from all direct political entanglements.

The Socialist Party itself, although it was nominally united, was as much divided by dissenting elements as its counterpart in Germany. The moderates, some of whose leaders had been expelled for following in the steps of Millerand, wanted to work with any party which would introduce a few reforms in return for socialist votes in the Chamber. The orthodox Marxists, though they had been converted to constitutional action, still refused to accept such co-operation as a matter of principle. The third group, led by Gustave Hervé, was strongly influenced by the doctrine of the syndicalists. At the head of the party stood Jaurès, who managed to hold the three groups together in an uneasy alliance on a platform of social reform, anti-militarism, State monopolies and—the reason for his assassination at the outbreak of war—friendship rather than hostility towards the German people.

When the war started, the breach between the socialists and the syndicalists had not been healed, and the experiences of the war years were to produce new and even more bitter divisions within the labour movement. But although the syndicalists never staged their general strike, and though they were slowly won over to less drastic methods, they made an important contribution to socialist theory. Like the Guild Socialists in England, on whom they exerted considerable influence, they called attention to the danger and inadequacy of a bureaucratic State socialism, and they revealed the potentialities of the trade unions, as both a weapon in the class-struggle and as the core round which the structure of a future economic democracy might be built—a doctrine that was paralleled by that of the Industrial Workers of the World in the U.S.A. In their emphasis on the need for a militant minority to lead the working-class, and for the workers to be represented as producers rather than as citizens, they anticipated the communists' belief that their party should be a vanguard of devoted revolutionaries and that a hierarchy of soviets—or workers' councils—should replace a central parliament as the means of government.

CHAPTER XII

LENIN AND THE BOLSHEVIKS

THROUGHOUT the nineteenth century, every liberal and democrat in Europe regarded Tsarist Russia as the bulwark of reaction: every autocrat considered the Tsar his natural ally, whose troops might be used to bolster up a tottering régime. There was widespread sympathy for the repeated but unsuccessful Polish revolts. To the West, Russia seemed a barbarous tyranny which stood on the fringe of civilization. Until 1861 the serfs were still the personal property of their masters. After that date the free peasants were bled white by landlords and moneylenders; national and racial minorities were incited to persecute each other; there was no industrial development of any importance until nearly the end of the century; and a vast army of bureaucrats and spies was employed to secure obedience to the edicts of the Tsar and his attendant aristocracy. Criticism led to foreign exile, Siberia, or the gallows. There was scarcely any political or intellectual freedom.

In this backward and ramshackle empire, effective and organized opposition could be expected only from one source —the educated class. It is true that there were recurrent peasant disturbances, but these were mostly local and spontaneous, lacking any of the elements which could have transformed them into a general uprising except the desperate hatred of men who found their misery unbearable.

The intelligentzia, however, was strongly influenced by the ideas and events of Western Europe. The students, writers, poets and some of the younger officers had studied the literature and the philosophy of the West, especially of France and Germany. They could not fail to contrast the sordid and despotic system under which they lived with the liberties enjoyed in the world beyond the frontiers of Russia.

Some of them, like Bakunin and Kropotkin, became prominent figures in the international revolutionary movement. Those that remained in Russia were constantly persecuted by the police. For all their brilliance and their courage, they could accomplish little as long as they remained a tiny isolated group without mass support. After 1873, when the Tsar recalled hundreds of students from abroad, there was a brief period in which the intellectuals "went to the people", living with them and trying to teach them the new ideas which they imported from the West. But this activity had not much success. The people found the greatest difficulty in understanding what these political missionaries were talking about. The Tsarist police, moreover, arrested thousands of them in an effort to stop their propaganda before it became really dangerous.

In the absence of any large-scale popular movement, which could be directed against the authorities, the Narodniks (literally "Party of the People"), as the revolutionaries were called, fell back upon conspiracy and terrorism as the only means of securing the changes they desired. They were dominated by anarchist doctrine and translated Bakunin's belief in the value of violence into practice. A whole series of assassinations culminated in the murder of Tsar Alexander II in March 1881. But this act did not touch off a general rising. The Terrorists optimistically expected an insurrection, but they had done nothing to prepare one. On the contrary, it provoked a new campaign of repression against democrats and socialists of all kinds.

It was clear that sporadic violence was no more likely to break up the Tsarist régime than was peaceful propaganda. But most of the Narodniks had no idea what they should do next. They did not believe that society developed according to a definite pattern. History for them was made by the heroism of outstanding individuals and not by the struggle of classes. Capitalism, which had appeared in Russia by accident, had no future. It followed from this that the proletariat, which was still small and ill-organized, could be ignored by the intelligentzia and the peasantry, which were the only revolutionary elements that mattered. Socialism, the Narodniks were convinced, would eventually be built on the traditional peasant commune. This position was understandable enough in a country where a vast peasant population was held in control, for centuries, by a bureaucracy wholly sub-servient to a central and absolute authority. The Narodniks naturally believed that by eliminating the leading figures of the régime the peasantry would gain their freedom. They were aware, at least, of the immense difficulties that had to be faced before socialism could be established in a nation of peasants (difficulties that made Marx himself sceptical of the possibility of successful revolution in Russia), and sought to avoid them by basing socialism upon the peasant community rather than, as in Western Europe, on the urban workers.

One section of the Narodnik movement, however, had realized that this policy led into a blind alley, and it turned towards Marxism. Under the leadership of Plekhanov the Marxists founded the Society for the Emancipation of Labour in 1883. They were at once engaged in a furious controversy with the remaining Narodniks. They insisted that capitalism was already well estabished in Russia; that the task of the revolutionaries was not to try to arrest its development but to provide a leadership for the growing working-class it had produced; and that it was absurd to regard the peasant com-mune—which was dominated by the wealthy farmers—as the embryonic form of socialism. But though these early Marxists had a far better understanding of the forces at work in Russia than the Narodniks, they did very little practical work among the proletarians on whom they staked their hopes. Their activity was almost entirely confined to the organization of study circles and they played no part in the strike wave of the 'eighties.

Among the young revolutionaries who belonged to these Marxist circles was Vladimir Ilyich Ulyanov, who adopted the pseudonym of Lenin. He was born in the town of Simbirsk in 1870, the son of a school inspector. His brother was hanged for complicity in a plot to assassinate the Tsar and he himself had to leave Kazan University for seditious activity. By the time Lenin arrived in St. Petersburg in 1893 he already had a close knowledge of Marxism, and two years later he helped to unite all the Marxist groups in the city into a League of Struggle. This body was the first in Russia to pass from mere propaganda to agitation among the working-class, linking socialist philosophy to the immediate demands of the misery-ridden workers.

Although many members of the League were arrested, it succeeded in organizing a number of important strikes and in stimulating the development of similar groups in many parts of Russia. But it was still impossible to weld these together into a single party. The congress which met at Minsk in 1898 for this purpose was attended by only nine delegates, who were arrested soon afterwards. The Russian Social-Democratic Labour Party had been founded in name only.

The Marxists made slow progress for the next few years. At the same time as they were striving to destroy the influence of the Narodniks, they had to fight against a new tendency that had appeared. This tendency, expressed by a group known as the "Economists", was to insist that the workers should concentrate their efforts on the economic struggle with the employers and should leave political matters to the liberals and the democrats. The "Economists", in fact, used virtually the same arguments against the formation of an independent party of workers as were used, with far more justification, in England. For although the English working-class had a great deal to gain by creating its own party, it was at least living under a constitutional government. The Russian proletariat, on the contrary, was denied even the most elementary rights and, as Lenin saw, it had nothing to lose by adopting illegal revolutionary methods.

But Lenin was in exile in Siberia and he could do little but plan for the future. It was during this period that he conceived the idea of starting a secret Marxist paper which, circulated on a large scale, would serve as a focus for the scattered Marxist groups, and as a major weapon in the ideological conflict with the Narodniks and the "Economists". As soon as he was permitted to return from Siberia, Lenin went abroad to arrange for the production of this paper, which was called *Iskra* (*The Spark*). The first issue was published in December 1900.

By this time there were nearly three million industrial workers in Russia, and though they were still a small fraction of the whole population, it was obvious that the Marxists had been right when they insisted that the proletariat would become the most militant and consistent revolutionary force in the country. In the first three years of the new century, which were marked by a serious commercial crisis, hundreds of thousands of workers were involved in strikes.

In these strikes, which were mostly led by the Marxists, the workers put forward political as well as economic demands. The revolutionary movement was gaining ground, but there was still no organized party which could link these local strikes together or provide an effective leadership for the developing alliance of the proletariat and the peasantry against their common enemy the Tsarist régime.

Before such a party could be built there had to be some sort of agreement about its structure and the principles upon which it was to be based. In the columns of *Iskra*, and in his book, *What Is To Be Done?*, Lenin insisted that the Russian Social-Democratic Labour Party could not be content to wait placidly until the workers spontaneously accepted socialist ideas. It had, on the contrary, to turn itself into a well-disciplined body of professional revolutionaries which would be capable of leading the proletariat steadfastly towards the conquest of power. Lenin did not want a party of reformists which would act as a parliamentary opposition once constitutional rights had been wrested from the Tsar. He believed that it was the mission of the Russian working-class to come forward as the champion of all the oppressed and exploited, to lead the peasants, the national and the racial minorities.

But Lenin's views were not shared by all those who wished to form a socialist party, in spite of the great influence exercised by *Iskra*. When, in 1903, a party congress was held in Brussels and then in London—really its inaugural congress, which, for reasons of safety, could not meet in Russia—the basic theoretical differences in the party found expression in a bitter dispute about its rules and programme. There were forty-three delegates present. Only twenty-four of them stood squarely behind Lenin. The remainder were vacillating moderates or else, like the three "Economists" and the five representatives of the Jewish Bund, open opponents of the policy advocated by Lenin in *Iskra*.

Nevertheless, after a heated debate, Lenin succeeded in pushing through his draft of a party programme. This committed the social-democrats, on paper at least, to the struggle for: first, a democratic republic; and second, the dictatorship of the proletariat. But what mattered, as Lenin realized, was not the willingness of the delegates to accept a general statement of aims. The test of their sincerity to the cause of the revolution was the nature of the party they were prepared to create in order to win power. It was on this issue that the congress split.

Martov, one of the most prominent Russian Marxists, wished to admit anyone to the party who agreed with its aims, even if they were not willing to do active work for it. He wanted a loose democratic organization, open to any sympathizer, which would function in much the same way as the socialist parties of Western Europe. Lenin, however, insisted that party membership was a vocation; that the mark of a genuine revolutionary was his whole-hearted devotion to the party; and that, consequently, he should accept an iron discipline. Nothing else, he insisted, would ensure the survival of the party under conditions of terror and illegality, such as it faced in Russia, let alone its final victory in the turmoil of a revolution. In between congresses, which were the highest authority of the party, its members should follow the orders of the elected Central Committee. In moments of crisis there would be neither time nor opportunity to undertake a consultation of the whole membership after the fashion of legal parties in the West. If Martov's proposal was adopted, the party would be opened to all sorts of rabble who could contribute nothing but confusion and who might actually destroy it. When the matter came to a vote, Lenin was defeated. But this defeat did not settle the matter, as the "Economists" and the members of the Bund withdrew from the congress after a dispute on another issue. This tipped the balance in Lenin's favour once more. In the vote for the Central Committee and for the editorial board of *Iskra* Lenin's supporters were elected. It was from the voting on these two questions that the two rival sections of the party took the names by which they have since been called. The majority, from the Russian word *bolshinstvo*, were known as the Bolsheviks. Martov's group, the minority, became the Mensheviks.

The voting at the London congress was too close to settle the dispute one way or the other, and once the split had taken place on this formal issue the two sections of the party found themselves at loggerheads on a number of fundamental questions. The Bolsheviks were unable to maintain the advantage they had secured in London. By winning over a few key individuals, particularly Plekhanov, the Mensheviks secured control both of *Iskra* and of the Central Committee. The Bolsheviks thereupon issued a new paper and set up a central body to organize their own supporters. Thus, on the eve of the Russian revolution of 1905 there were two distinct groups, nominally united, but each possessing its own organization and policy, and each claiming that it alone should act as the leadership of the working-class.

Nobody planned the revolution of 1905. It was the outcome of the disastrous defeats in the Russo-Japanese war, coming as they did on top of a serious economic depression. Popular indignation with the incompetent conduct of the war and with the frightful casualties suffered by the Russian armies coincided with a new wave of strikes, many of them led by the Bolsheviks. On January 9th, 1905, a vast procession of workers marched to the Winter Palace in St. Petersburg to present a petition to the Tsar. They demanded freedom of speech and organization, the convocation of a constituent assembly, division of Church and State, the grant of land to the peasants and peace with Japan. Nicholas II answered their requests by ordering the police and troops to open fire. At least one thousand workers were shot.

This massacre was the signal for disturbances all over Russia. In January alone more than five hundred thousand workers went on strike. For several months there were strikes, riots and street fighting in the big towns. The peasants rose in one district after another, burning the houses and seizing the land of their masters. In June the sailors on the battleship *Potemkin* mutinied and sailed away to Rumania. The revolutionary movement was spreading rapidly.

But what sort of revolution was it? The Mensheviks and

the Bolsheviks had different answers to this question when each group held its own congress early in 1905. It was, said the Mensheviks, a liberal-democratic revolution and should, therefore, be led by the liberals and the democrats and not by the workers. It was necessary for the proletariat to act with restraint and to refrain from extreme demands in case it frightened the middle-class away from the revolution altogether. Socialism was not immediately possible in Russia, since the country was backward economically. The workers, therefore, should not take part in any provisional government that might be formed and should leave the task of drafting a constitution to the liberal parties. The Bolsheviks, however, were not prepared to accommodate their tactics to the timidity of their liberal allies. These, the Bolsheviks argued, were only interested in winning limited concessions and were much more afraid of the workers and peasants than of the Tsarist régime. It was the duty of the working-class to push the revolution as far as it could, because it required the conditions of political democracy in order to complete its preparations for the next stage of the struggle.

Lenin, in fact, had already worked out the essential features of the strategy that was to carry the Bolsheviks to victory only a few years later. He did not accept the Menshevik view that it was necessary for Russia to pass through a fairly long period of industrial capitalist development, at the end of which the workers would somehow seize power. He believed that, for a number of reasons, it was possible in Russia to go straight on from the bourgeois to the proletarian revolution without any need for a pause. It was thus necessary for the working-class to isolate the liberals and to assume the leadership of the movement as quickly as it could. Moreover, unlike the socialists of the West, who regarded the peasants as an obstacle to progress, Lenin realized that they were the natural allies of the proletariat and that the conquest of power was impossible without their co-operation. He therefore sought to forge a close alliance between the two classes which would fight against the Tsarist Government and neutralize the liberals. Owing to the late and distorted development of capitalism in Russia, the struggle against autocracy and the struggle for socialism had overlapped.

While the socialists were deciding what attitude they should adopt towards the revolution, it was spreading with increasing speed. In October a huge strike occurred, involving more than a million industrial workers, apart from the employees of the railway and postal services. It was in the course of this strike that the soviets (or councils of workers) made their first appearance. They were formed by delegates elected directly from factories and other enterprises and acted, for a short time, as the effective authority in the towns where they were set up, introducing freedom of the press and, in some cases, confiscating State taxes for their own revolutionary purposes. The strike wrung promises of reform from the Tsar, including a general franchise and a legislative assembly.

These concessions, the Bolsheviks said, showed that the old régime was unable to govern any longer by the old methods. But they were not enough. A final armed uprising was necessary to overthrow the tottering system. The revolt started in Moscow in December 1905. It was accompanied by strikes and uprisings from Finland to the Ukraine and Georgia. But the Tsarist Government was still strong enough to suppress the scattered insurrection, and thousands of revolutionaries were killed in the fighting, or executed, or thrown into prison. For months, punitive expeditions scoured Poland, Siberia, Transcaucasia and the Baltic provinces. The revolutionary tide had turned. There were a number of revolts in the years after 1906, but the chance had been lost once the opposition parties, apart from the Bolsheviks, had refused to resort to arms and had left the revolutionaries to their fate.

Though the Tsar kept his promise and convened a Duma, or legislative assembly, its powers were limited and its life was short. As soon as it began to make any definite demands it was forcibly dissolved. Its successor suffered the same fate. The electoral law was then revised in order to increase the number of representatives who supported the Tsar, one deputy being elected by every two hundred nobles and one by every hundred thousand workers. This new Duma sat throughout the period of reaction that lasted until 1912. It tolerated the imprisonment of no less than two hundred members of the First Duma and the Second Duma—in which the revolutionaries had not even participated—the execution of thousands and the banishment of about two hundred thousand people to Siberia.

Inside the socialist movement, which found it difficult to keep going at all under this reign of terror, there was still a bitter theoretical struggle between the two rival sections. The Mensheviks were demanding that there should be no illegal revolutionary work on the grounds that this was endangering the whole existence of the party. They wanted to confine their activity to socialist education and to such methods as were still tolerated. The Bolsheviks, however, insisted that the party should go on steadily preparing for insurrection so that the opportunity would not be lost a second time. In spite of the severe difficulties under which they had to work, they managed to hold their supporters together. Finally, at the congress of the social-democrats in Prague, in 1912, they formally expelled the Mensheviks and Lenin at last had his united and disciplined party of professional revolutionaries.

From 1912 onwards the revolutionary revival began to resemble the course of events that had preceded the outbreak of 1905. The shooting of five hundred strikers in the Lena goldfields in Siberia touched off a new series of mass strikes and political demonstrations. All over Russia, under Bolshevik leadership, there was unrest among the workers, peasants and the armed forces. But this time the strikers were demanding a new revolution, not reforms. The Bolsheviks were still outnumbered by the other opposition parties, which ranged from the Mensheviks on the Left to the peasant Social-Revolutionaries and the Constitutional Democrats on the Right. But they were the most militant and best-organized of them all. The Russian socialist movement was no more united than its counterparts in the West, but in Russia it was at least clear which groups stood for constitutional reform and which for revolution on the Marxist model.

The outbreak of the war threw the European socialists into confusion. Most of the parties supported it from the start and only later began to consider whether they could do anything to bring it to an end. In Russia the Bolsheviks realized that it would mean a temporary setback until the masses learnt through their own suffering that the war was nothing more than an imperialist conflict. Then, they believed, their chance would come and they would be able to bring the uneasy partnership between capitalism and the autocracy tumbling down in ruins. It was an omen that there were barricades on the streets of St. Petersburg at the moment war was being declared.

CHAPTER XIII

THE SECOND INTERNATIONAL AND THE WAR

By the outbreak of the World War in 1914 socialism had become a considerable force in European politics. The most striking progress had been made, as we have seen, in France and Germany, where there were large working-class parties which counted their supporters by the hundred thousand. But all over the Continent socialist organizations of some kind had been set up and had begun to play a part in the affairs of their respective countries. There were parties even in Argentina and the United States, where Eugene Debs, the socialist candidate for the Presidency, polled nearly 900,000 votes in the elections of 1912.

Though all these movements had adapted themselves with some success to the specific national conditions under which they had to work, this did not mean that the idea of international action had been forgotten. On the contrary, a new body had been formed to take the place of the old First International and to co-ordinate, as far as possible, the policies and work of its affiliated parties. Most of these were strongly influenced by Marxism and, nominally at least, were committed to the doctrine of the unity of the workers of all lands against capitalism and against war. But, as the World War was to reveal, this sense of unity was not strong enough to hold the movement together once the workers were called upon to defend their native land. Nationalism then took precedence over socialism.

The Belgian socialist leader, Emile Vandervelde, once described the First International as a brilliant general staff without an army. Its successor, however, possessed an army of millions but lacked an effective general staff. From its birth as an organized centre in 1901—though there had been occasional congresses before this—until it disintegrated in 1914, the Second International never had any real power to control the parties which belonged to it. Since it was open to any group which accepted the broad principles of socialism, regardless of the doctrine on which it was based, it served primarily as a forum in which questions of general and theoretical interest were discussed. From time to time it did intervene in the activities of the socialists in particular countries—in France, for instance, it was instrumental in unifying the rival parties in 1905—but, even if it had wished to do so, it could not have issued orders and received unquestioning obedience from so large and so loose an organization.

It is true that the decisions of its successive congresses were sometimes accepted by individuals or by parties which disagreed with them, but this secured formal rather than real agreement. The size of the International was a deceptive measure of its strength. It was little more than a numerical aggregate of its constituent parties. As such its proceedings reflected the theoretical and practical differences which divided these parties themselves. The struggle between the reformists and the revolutionaries, to take the most fundamental issue, was fought out as bitterly at the congresses of the International as within the ranks of the various national parties.

But, in a period of comparative peace, when socialists appeared to be making steady progress everywhere, this structural weakness did not seem to matter very much. The leaders of the Second International proved to their own satisfaction that as long as they continued to act as a central clearing-house, publishing detailed and valuable reports on the activities of the various parties and on social problems of general concern, they were doing virtually all that was required of them.

Numbers, for them, were the important thing. As good parliamentary politicians, they measured their success in terms of the votes they commanded and not, as did Lenin and the other radical Marxists, by the discipline and unity of their supporters. In the same way they were well satisfied with the International because it had affiliated sections all the way from Portugal to Armenia and Norway to Bulgaria. Nothing, they felt, could now frustrate the advance of this invincible army. Each year brought it closer to victory. Even in distant Australia there had been a minority Labour Government—the first in the world—in 1904, while in nearby New Zealand the Labour Party was sufficiently strong to take part in a coalition with the Liberals before the nineteenth century reached its end. Socialism, it was true, was still a minority movement, but only time was needed to remedy that.

This attitude, we can see today, was based on an illusion, but it accounts for the extraordinary contrast between the apparent strength and unity of the Second International and its collapse almost overnight in the summer of 1914. It had devoted a good deal of time to debating the attitude of socialists towards war. In 1907, at a congress in Stuttgart, a famous resolution was carried which urged the workers to do everything in their power to prevent a conflict. If they were unable to do this, they were to try and bring it quickly to an end and to use the resulting economic and political crisis to rouse the people and thus hasten the downfall of capitalism. At the Copenhagen Congress in 1910 another resolution instructed socialist representatives to vote against the war credits of their respective governments.

Two years later, at Basle, more than five hundred delegates supported a motion declaring that it was a crime for workers of various countries to shoot one another for the sake of increasing the profits of the capitalists. There was, it would seem, very little doubt about the question. The policy had been thrashed out openly and a majority of the socialist parties had endorsed it. But if they had taken the resolutions seriously they would have begun to prepare for a hard revolutionary struggle. It was typical of most of the parties belonging to the Second International that they did nothing of the kind, although they were perfectly willing to accept, in theory, decisions which could not mean anything else.

In the last weeks of July 1914, when it was clear that war was imminent, attempts were made to implement the policy to which the Second International was committed. But it was then too late. On the 29th of July, while the leaders of the European socialist parties were meeting in Paris to consider how they could prevent the war, the powerful Austrian party

I

had already decided to support the attack on Serbia. Müller, one of the German representatives, who announced that his party would not under any circumstances vote for war credits, returned to Berlin just in time to join his comrades in voting for the first credit of ten milliard marks. In France, Jean Jauèrs was assassinated two days after he had called for opposition to the war, and on the day he was buried the socialists in the Chamber unanimously decided to enter the Government until Imperial Germany was crushed. The same story was true of Belgium.

The British Labour Party, though a section of the party, including Hardie and MacDonald, was anti-war, decided to give conditional support for the Liberal Government's decision to fight. Only the tiny party in Serbia and the Russian Bolsheviks took their stand on the Stuttgart and Basle resolutions. The Second International was in ruins.

There was, however, a minority in each of the larger parties which opposed the war and denounced the majority sections for betraying the fundamental socialist principles of internationalism and anti-militarism. In some cases, like the I.L.P. in England, this minority was pacifist rather than revolutionary, but in general the division followed much the same lines as the pre-war cleavage between the reformists and orthodox Marxists. These groups managed to hold an international conference at Zimmerwald in 1915. Apart from Lenin and the other Bolsheviks living in exile in Switzerland, all the thirty-three delegates represented countries that were either neutral or fighting on the side of Germany. At this conference, and at its successor held in the village of Kienthal a year later, manifestos were drafted denouncing the war as the outcome of imperialism and capitalist rivalry, and urging the immediate conclusion of peace without annexations or indemnities. But at neither conference did the Bolsheviks succeed in winning a majority for Lenin's thesis that socialists should seek to turn the imperialist war into a civil war, should work for the defeat and overthrow of their own governments, and should decisively break with the moderates and reformists who supported the war, forming a new and revolutionary Third International.

These proposals seemed too drastic at a time when there was still no widespread opposition to the war among the workers of the belligerent nations and when the major Powers seemed capable of continuing the war indefinitely.

But the deadlock was broken more quickly than anyone expected. By the beginning of 1917 Russia was exhausted. The Tsarist régime was unable to suppress the discontent in the defeated and decimated armies or in the big towns. The Empire of Nicholas II was falling to pieces and there was nobody able or willing to hold it together. In March the troops who were called out to put down a mass political strike in Petrograd refused to obey orders, and joined the workers in the streets. Within two days the struggle was over in Petrograd, and the revolution had spread throughout Russia and to the armies at the front. Hungry, disillusioned and miserable, the subjects of the Tsarist régime had risen and destroyed it.

But what had taken its place? Everyone, from the liberals to the Bolsheviks, agreed that the March victory had at last completed the democratic revolution which began in 1905. Autocracy had been overthrown, and it seemed to liberal observers that Russia might gradually develop along the same lines as the countries of the West.

The Provisional Government, which had been set up by the Fourth Duma, promised to convene a constituent assembly to draft a new political structure and to carry on the war at the side of the Allies. In this it was supported by a majority in the Workers' and Soldiers' Soviets, which had sprung up rapidly and which were, at this time, under the leadership of the Mensheviks and the Social-Revolutionaries. But the Bolsheviks alone insisted that the revolution which started in March must be continued until the Provisional Government, dominated by representatives of big business and Russia's small middle-class, had itself been replaced by an alliance of peasants and workers. The collapse of the Tsarist régime, the Bolsheviks argued, did not automatically change the war from an imperialist to a progressive conflict.

Soon after the first revolution Lenin returned to Russia from Switzerland. He found that his own party was divided about the war. In fact, most of his adherents who met him at the station on the April night that he arrived in Petrograd (Leningrad today) were startled by the violence with which he denounced any attempt to continue the war as merely a continuation, by pseudo-revolutionaries, of the aggressive purposes of the Russian bourgeoisie. Lenin had to fight hard against even his closest friends and adherents in order to swing the Bolsheviks wholeheartedly behind his policy of "revolutionary defeatism". The Russian people, he argued, had nothing to gain from continued participation in the struggle. Alexander Kerensky, the dominant figure in the succession of provisional governments that held power precariously through the summer of 1917, might insist that the war had become a war of defence in which the Russians sought no more than the protection of their frontiers and the fulfilment of their commitments to the Allies. As far as Lenin was concerned, Kerensky insisted in vain. The more lives that were squandered in futile offensives, the more the Bolsheviks raised the cry of peace at any price. As long as Russia continued to associate with the Allies, the war remained imperialist and it was the duty of a revolutionary to stimulate disaffection and unrest and to work—whether he was a German or a Russian, Lenin reiterated—for the defeat of his own government.

If it was difficult for Lenin to carry his own party with him, it was equally hard for the Bolsheviks to escape the charge of treachery. Tardy repression, indeed, did drive the party underground as the summer wore on, but too late to save the Kerensky régime. For Russia was disintegrating under the blows of the German army, under the pressure of military mutiny, of peasants hungry for land and peace, of insurgent and ill-fed urban workers, and of the national minorities for whom, in Lenin's phrase, Russia was a "prison-house". The Bolsheviks, few though they were at this time, were able to exploit every tension to their advantage. The more their opponents rallied round the increasingly inept and unpopular Provisional Government, the better the Bolsheviks could isolate them from a people which was war-weary and hungry. The peasants, Lenin said, "voted with their feet". They would fight no longer —and the Bolsheviks, as the peace party, reaped the benefits of their anger and exhaustion.

Lenin, of course, was running enormous risks by this policy. It was one thing to call for peace as a revolutionary tactic against a war government: it was a different matter when the revolution itself might be endangered by total defeat at the hands of the German army. Yet Lenin counted on revolution inside Germany coming to the aid of Russia and, in any case, he believed that if the Bolsheviks supported the war they would lose the chief attraction their policy possessed: the desire for peace. Support of the war would have meant the end of Bolshevik hopes for a further revolution that would put them in power. Lenin knew this, and knew also that if he missed this chance to push through the seizure of power in 1917 it might not occur again for a long time. The times were ripe. Whatever the hazards, the Bolsheviks had to push on. A Bolshevik march was broken up by troops in July. This disheartened some of Lenin's comrades, but merely increased his determination to succeed. From the hiding-place to which he had fled from Kerensky's police, just across the Finnish border, Lenin directed a stream of letters and pamphlets at the Bolshevik Central Committee, denouncing those who drew back from another uprising as traitors, weaklings and incompetents.

At last, early in November (October 24th, by the Russian calendar), plans were complete, though at the last minute such leading Bolsheviks as Zinoviev and Kamenev objected that the revolt was a wild and doomed folly. Lenin knew what he wanted. He had bullied and cajoled his party into the desperate attempt. On November 7th insurgent groups seized Petrograd after a very short struggle. Moscow fell soon after. The Provisional Government was dissolved and the Bolsheviks, with some allies from the Left of the other parties, proclaimed themselves the rulers of Russia. Lenin, in the face of apparently insuperable obstacles, had carried through his proletarian revolution. He had never believed that socialism could be achieved by electoral successes, least of all in Russia, where even free speech and assembly had been wanting until the overthrow of the Tsarist régime. Defeat in war had given him his chance, and when, as he said, "power fell into our hands like a ripe fruit", he made sure that he had armed force enough to hold it.

All the other parties, from the Mensheviks to the liberals, denounced the revolt as treachery and tyranny, but they could do little about it. Their day was over. They had to choose between support of the Bolshevik régime and the counter-revolution. In Russia, at least, the dispute about the methods the workers should adopt to win power was no longer a theoretical issue. It had been settled in the streets of Petrograd in favour of the Marxist revolutionaries. While the reformists debated, the Bolsheviks had armed. For more than ten years Lenin had insisted that Russia would be able to pass straight from the bourgeois to the proletarian revolution. When the troops of the Revolutionary Military Committee, led by Leon Trotsky, established the first communist government in the world, they brought to pass the Marxist prophecy in the one country of which the Marxists, from Marx himself to Lenin, had previously had least hope. Russia, as Lenin said that evening, would proceed to the inauguration of socialism.

This, however, was no easy task. The peasants had quickly taken the land they desired. But there was widespread hunger; the resources of the country had been squandered in the war; industry was almost at a standstill; there was chaos everywhere and in everything. Yet the peace Lenin had demanded could not be secured as easily as the estates of landlords. Germany would not easily relinquish her hopes of vast plunder from a defeated Russia nor her demands for territorial satisfaction, especially in the Ukraine. While the negotiations dragged on at Brest-Litovsk the Bolsheviks found themselves forced to continue a fighting retreat. At times, when the German terms seemed outrageous, Lenin was in a minority on the Bolshevik Central Committee, most of whose members—including Trotsky—preferred to fight on rather than accept an intolerable peace. But Lenin was adamant. Any terms short of the actual destruction of the Bolshevik régime had to be accepted, to give the new state a breathing-space, in which it could be both consolidated and rehabilitated.

Eventually the Bolsheviks signed a peace treaty with Germany at Brest-Litovsk. While this treaty awarded the Germans a large part of Russia—it was all to be recovered after the German collapse—and permitted them to move a large part of their troops away from the Russian front to Western Europe, it is unlikely that the Bolshevik régime would have survived but for the chance this temporary peace gave it to consolidate. For within a few months, counter-revolution, aided by the Germans and by the Allies, had broken out in various parts of Russia. The remnants of the Tsarist army, joined both by wealthy landlords and merchants as well as opponents of Bolshevism ranging as far to the Left as Social Revolutionaries and Mensheviks, were in arms against the young Soviet Republic, holding huge areas of the country. They imposed a "White Terror", backed by foreign troops, arms and money, to which the Bolsheviks reacted in turn. The Civil War merged into the War of Intervention—the memory of which still lingers in Russia today as a barrier to friendly relations with the outside world.

At one time the Bolsheviks held only a comparatively small part of Russia around Petrograd and Moscow. It seemed that the Bolsheviks would inevitably be crushed. They were not. Their iron discipline held the régime together: if they won there was the chance of building a new society. If they lost, as many people who had little sympathy with their more extreme proposals realized, Russia would drift rapidly into ruin and the old aristocrats and landlords would come back behind the White armies and the troops of the capitalist Powers who were fighting against the Bolsheviks. Better the uncertain though rosy future promised by the Marxists than a return to the old misery. It was this combination of hope and desperation that rallied the people of Russia and the former oppressed nations and sustained the improvised Red Army in its struggle on seventeen different fronts simultaneously. For a time the Bolsheviks introduced a system of military communism, in which every aspect of life was subordinated to the central authority in the effort to survive.

After the war against the Whites and the Allied armies of intervention had been won, Russia needed a breathing-space to restore the dreadful losses of the past seven years. The Bolsheviks then, under the New Economic Policy, relaxed some of the restrictions on small business and on private farming, though they still kept the large industries under State ownership and control.

During the war years, however, all this lay in the future. Very few people in Russia, let alone in the outside world, had any idea of the course events were to take. The Bolsheviks appeared in the West as a handful of desperadoes, probably subsidized by the Germans, who had taken Russia out of the war and—what seemed far more dangerous—had expropriated the capitalists and landlords according to the traditional Marxist programme. These fears were encouraged by the constant appeals that the Bolsheviks made to the workers of the Powers that were still at war, urging them to follow the Russian example, to overthrow their rulers and to make a just peace.

In these years Lenin was convinced that the revolution would spread. He regarded the victory in Russia as merely the prelude to the bigger and more bitter struggle that would come in the more advanced industrial countries. Russia was the base for this inevitable conflict. The links which held the capitalist world together had been broken at their weakest point. Soon, he believed, the workers of the world would finally unite for the last fight of which they had sung so often in the *Internationale*. Though there was little contact between the rest of Europe and blockaded Russia, enough was known of the revolution for the workers elsewhere to realize that, in some way, their comrades were the masters of a great country, that there was a practical way of ending the suffering caused by the war and, at the same time, of winning power for themselves.

The revolutionary groups which had all along opposed the war naturally acclaimed the Bolshevik victory. But it also evoked a response even from the moderates, who were increasingly uneasy about a war they had once, in every country, enthusiastically supported. Though they disliked the methods of the Bolsheviks and were not at all anxious to be involved in similar activities themselves, they could not acquiesce in the destruction of the first successful socialist revolution.

Lenin regarded this foreign sympathy as one of the chief assets of the Bolsheviks. To co-ordinate it, and to provide a rallying-point for the growing revolutionary movement, he and the Bolsheviks formed the Third International. This, unlike its predecessor, was intended to act as a general staff for the proletariat of the world. It was to be highly disciplined; all its member parties were to base themselves uncompromisingly on the Leninist interpretation of Marxism; and it was to admit only those groups and individuals who had cut themselves off from the old reformist parties which, Lenin insisted, had disgraced themselves by supporting an imperialist war.

In vitriolic language the Bolsheviks denounced the moderates for leading the working-class into an impasse. They had encouraged illusions about peaceful change; they had betrayed the workers who had trusted them by entering into disgraceful alliances with their own capitalists against their fellow-workers in other countries; and finally, when the supreme opportunity had arrived, they were too comfortable and too timid to seize it. Did they want socialism or not? Did they imagine that the greatest social change in history could be accomplished by agreement with the very class that had to be overthrown? The war was not a terrible accident. It was the inevitable product of imperialist rivalries. Unless the capitalist system were liquidated there would be a whole series of such world wars, each succeeded by a more calamitous economic crisis. Certainly, bloodshed would be necessary to establish socialism. But the cost would be small compared with the suffering and destruction that would follow if capitalism were allowed to continue. The working-class movement must not shirk its responsibilities now that the old society had begun to disintegrate.

The Bolshevik appeals began to yield results. In France an important section of the Socialist Party had begun to vote systematically against war measures, to demand a compromise peace and support for the Russian revolution. Army mutinies were accompanied by strikes in the factories.

The same was true, though on a larger scale, in Germany, where the most extreme elements in the Social-Democratic Party had moved almost to the Bolshevik position. Even in England there was widespread industrial unrest, particularly on the "Red" Clyde, and even before the Bolshevik revolt, though after the first (February) Revolution a completely futile

attempt had been made to form a national network of councils
on the soviet model. In every belligerent country there was
a profound weariness and growing opposition to a continuation of the war. By the end of 1917 the revolutionaries were
no longer an isolated sect.

Throughout the late summer of 1918 Germany was rapidly
approaching the end of its resources. Apart from the workers, a
large part of the peasantry and sections of the middle-class
were demanding peace. The Government was unable to check
the great strikes in the munition industries called by the extreme
Left. The Social-Democratic leaders, however, still regarded
it as their duty to fight on, though they made continued support of the war conditional upon the immediate introduction
of certain reforms and the conclusion of a peace which restored
the independence of Belgium and the territories filched from
Russia by the onerous treaty signed with the Bolsheviks at
Brest-Litovsk.

But, by November, nothing could save Germany. The
Allies had broken Hindenburg's army. The soldiers and
sailors were mutinying. Even before an armistice could be
secured and the Kaiser driven to abdicate, the revolution had
started and the troops had begun to join the workers in the
streets of Berlin, and other centres. For two or three days it
seemed that the extreme Left might win control. But the
moderate socialists had no intention of permitting an upheaval
on the Russian model. They quickly put themselves at the head
of the revolution and sought to limit its scope. Ebert, their
leader, was even reluctant to proclaim the end of the monarchy,
but his colleague, Phillip Scheidemann, fearing that Karl
Liebknecht and the revolutionary Marxists were about to
call for a communist republic, forestalled them by announcing
the substitution of a democratic republic for the dynasty. He
did this on his own initiative, much to the fury of Ebert,
who had been negotiating for the formation of a constitutional monarchy with one of the Kaiser's younger sons at
its head.

From the first, the moderates showed that they were more
terrified of the Left than of the Right. In a considerable part
of Germany local power was in the hands of revolutionary,

soviets. The communist groups and the bigger Independent Socialist Party, which had carried the non-Bolshevik but radical elements out of the main social-democratic organization, were demanding that the revolution be continued until the power of the ruling-class had been broken.

This was the last thing that the moderates wanted, for they could see themselves being swept away just as Kerensky had been pushed aside in Russia. If Germany fell into the hands of the communists, they believed, the Allies would occupy the whole country and dictate a ruinous peace. Germany, in any case, was not yet ripe for socialism: the huge vote they now commanded was not a vote for the expropriation of the capitalists but merely for social reforms. All that could be done, without disorganizing the whole economy of the country, was to limit the activities of monopolies and to establish a democratic capitalist State.

Some changes, of course, were necessary, but civil war, starvation and chaos would be unavoidable if order were not immediately restored and the reactionary parties were not reconciled to the gains that the revolution had already achieved. These arguments, naturally, did nothing but infuriate many of the workers. They saw the social-democratic leaders acting exactly as the Bolsheviks had predicted they would act, as the allies and defenders of capitalism at a moment when it appeared to be on the verge of collapse. Strikes, demonstrations and even street fighting followed.

Ebert, now President, had to fall back on the conservatives and the militarists for support. In fact, he actually made a secret alliance with Field-Marshal Hindenburg for common action against the communists. Hundreds of ex-officers, the forerunners of the Nazi storm troops, were mobilized into formations which could be used to suppress the revolutionary movement. In 1919 one of these squads murdered both Karl Liebknecht and Rosa Luxemburg. Terrified of Bolshevism, the moderate socialists rushed into the arms of the people who most hated both German democracy and German socialism. They did nothing to break the power of the Junkers or of the huge capitalist trusts. They split the working-class into two irreconcilable sections—a breach that was never healed and undoubtedly paved the way for the Nazi victory in 1933.

Their behaviour in these troubled years was one of the most tragic and discreditable episodes in the history of socialism. The extreme Left was not blameless. It, too, was responsible for serious mistakes—the communists clearly over-estimated the possibility of successful revolution against the alliance of the moderates and the German ruling-class. But, at least, they did not betray the basic principles of the whole socialist movement. There is no evidence that the social-democrats would have been more radical even if there had been no challenge on their Left.

Elsewhere in Europe, the war had ended in revolutionary outbreaks. The Austro-Hungarian Empire had disintegrated and its component nationalities had set up their own States. In Austria itself there was an abortive communist revolt, while Hungary, for a short time, became a Soviet Republic, led by Bela Kun. But this régime was soon suppressed by the Rumanian armies, backed by the victorious Allies. Though Poland had at last won independence, it had been drawn into the war against the Bolsheviks and had suppressed the revolutionary movement. Nowhere outside Russia, however, did the communists manage to repeat the Bolshevik success. By 1920 Lenin realized that the tide had turned and that there was no immediate possibility of an extension of the proletarian revolution to the West.

But, in spite of the failure of the European workers to follow the Russian example, the Bolsheviks were by no means isolated. The Communist International, with its headquarters in Moscow, was growing in importance as, in one country after another, disciplined parties consciously based on the Bolshevik model were formed by the revolutionaries. In Europe alone they claimed a membership of more than one million. One or two of the old socialist parties had affiliated to the Comintern as a whole; elsewhere a large section had broken away to set up a new communist organization. Communism, whatever setbacks it might temporarily encounter, had come to stay.

This clearly transformed the entire socialist movement. Until 1914 the moderates and the revolutionary Marxists had worked in an uneasy partnership within the ranks of nominally united parties. After the end of the war, that proved to be impossible. There had always been this cleavage between the two tendencies, from the moment that socialism had started to spread in Europe. The experiences of the war and its aftermath changed this difference into an open conflict. For the Marxists, the moderates were no longer comrades with mistaken views but were traitors whose influence on the masses was the most serious obstacle to the destined victory of the proletariat.

Conversely, the social-democrats denounced Bolshevism as tyranny and communism as a disruptive and ruinous tactic. They insisted that socialism had much more in common with liberal democracy than with the strange and seemingly ephemeral system that was being created in the East. If it came to a choice between winning power by force or remaining little more than a radical opposition in a capitalist society, they preferred the latter alternative. For, apart from the Left socialists, who stood midway between the communists and reformists, they still did not accept the Marxist thesis that capitalism had entered a period of crisis from which there was no escape save socialism. They saw no reason why things should not continue in much the same way as before the war, with a steady increase in the socialist vote and a gradual extension of State control over private enterprise. The only danger was that communist activity might provide an excuse for restrictive or even repressive action against the whole socialist and trade union movement. They attributed the shifts in communist policy to the strong and increasing control that the Russians, through the Comintern, exerted over the smaller member parties. This, they said, made communism little more than a mere instrument of Soviet foreign policy, which could be used at Moscow's discretion to aid the friends of the Stalin régime and to attack and embarrass its enemies. Bitter experience over the years had taught social-democrats—their argument ran—that when communists embraced them it was the better to strangle them. Though many socialists rejected this sceptical approach, the dominant groups in the socialist parties found fresh evidence with each new development of communist policy to support their critical thesis.

Thus, in the years after the First World War, the history of socialism is as much a record of rivalry between communism and social-democracy as of the larger struggle of the whole movement against capitalism. It was no longer enough to agree with the broad principles of socialism. The politically-minded worker had to choose between two competing methods of achieving power.

CHAPTER XIV

THE YEARS OF CRISIS

WITHIN two or three years of the end of the war between Germany and the Allies the socialist movement everywhere had settled down into a pattern that was to remain comparatively unaltered until the development of a powerful fascist conspiracy on an international scale created a serious threat to socialism, democracy and peace. It was some time before the rest of the world began to establish diplomatic and trading relations with Russia, but once it was clear that the Soviet régime could not be overthrown by foreign intervention, and was not going to collapse of its own accord, the Bolsheviks were left more or less alone—though everything possible was done to isolate them—to proceed with the construction of their new social system. They managed, however, to exercise a considerable influence on the workers of other countries, directly through the agency of the Comintern and its affiliated sections and, indirectly, by winning the sympathy of many socialists who regarded Russia as the first State run by the common people, even if these sympathizers were not themselves prepared to accept the whole Marxist doctrine as interpreted by Lenin.

In Germany, as we shall see below, there was a period of deadlock, in which the Left, divided into two warring camps, was too strong to be suppressed by the reaction and too weak to take power itself. In Finland, Poland and the Balkans there was a dictatorship of the Right, barely concealed behind a façade of parliamentary institutions. Czecho-Slovakia, forged out of the ruins of the Hapsburg Empire, had become a typical capitalist democracy.

In France and in Britain, which had both emerged from the war without serious internal upheavals and with their economic structure still intact, though shaken, the socialists found themselves working under much the same sort of social and political conditions as had prevailed before 1914, though their overall position was much stronger. Only in Italy, among the major States, had things taken a definite turn for the worse.

Italy, one of the weakest and most backward capitalist nations, had gained nothing of value from the war and had suffered a series of disastrous defeats. The only thing upon which the majority of Italian socialists agreed was opposition to the war. Apart from the division between the two Marxist tendencies, which existed all over Europe, the Italian labour movement had been strongly influenced by anarchism and syndicalism. When, immediately after the war, a revolutionary crisis developed, none of the various groups was itself strong enough to take the lead and none was willing to co-operate with its rivals. For a short time the workers in the North took matters into their own hands and occupied the factories. But there was no central leadership of any use and the incipient revolt petered out. The Italian Socialist Party first joined the Comintern and then quickly left it. On the Left, at a moment when everyone in Italy expected the workers to take power, there was only confusion.

It was an ideal situation for Mussolini, the former socialist journalist, and his newly-formed Fascist Party. The Italian middle-class, to say nothing of the landlords and capitalists, were terrified at the prospect of revolution, and they turned eagerly to a mass movement which seemed able to defend the interests of property. The fascists, moreover, appealed to the nationalist sentiments of a people which believed itself to have been cheated out of its legitimate reward for joining the Allies in the war. Using pseudo-socialist slogans, as the Nazis later did in Germany, they were able even to get some support from the workers, who were disillusioned by the quarrels and incapacity of the parties of the Left.

With the connivance of the ruling-class Mussolini was able to seize power without any difficulty and to proceed to the suppression of all opposition to the fascist régime. In this he had the full support of the Italian capitalists, who, once they were confronted with a serious socialist challenge, found that they had little use for the trappings of democracy. They had no hesitation at all in endorsing a brutal dictatorship, for this seemed to be the only thing that could guarantee their survival.

In these circumstances there was no point in the socialists debating the respective merits of peaceful reform or revolution. The question had been settled for them. After 1925, when the fascist régime was firmly consolidated, they had to face the prospect of long years of illegal struggle.

At first fascism appeared to be a phenomenon characteristic only of Italy. But in Germany a similar movement had begun to gain ground. In its humble beginnings in Bavaria the National Socialist German Workers' Party, led by Gregor Strasser and Adolf Hitler, did not seem very different from the scores of parties which had sprung up in the Weimar Republic, consisting mainly of war veterans who hated communism, the Jews and democracy with equal venom. Germany, these said, had been betrayed by this unholy trinity, which had led the country into defeat, economic ruin and political chaos. They formed armed bands which placed themselves at the disposal of anyone, even the socialist Minister, Noske, who would offer them the opportunity to shoot or otherwise terrorize the members of the growing communist movement.

The Social-Democratic Party leaders, who had been in a position of unquestioned authority immediately after the war, found themselves drifting into coalitions with the nationalists, the Catholic Party, and conservatives. Once they had decided to adopt a policy of compromise and conciliation they found it difficult to make a stand anywhere. There was a continual threat of insurrection (doomed, in the circumstances, to result in failure and further divisions among the German workers) from the communists, whose influence among the workers increased as the socialists tried to damp down trade union activity for fear it might hamper the revival of the German economy, as they called out the police and the *Reichswehr* to break up strikes and demonstrations, and as they seemed unable to take any decisive steps to change Germany into a socialist State.

All the time the reactionaries were regaining their strength and the monopolies were extendng their grip on the national economy with the assistance of the State. Most of the social-democrats, it is true, were perfectly happy at the course of events and lived in a perpetual illusion that Germany was moving steadily towards democratic socialism. But by 1931 a minority had come to realize that their party was in an intolerable position. Paralysed by the fear of Bolshevism, it had watched the Nazis, who had become the most powerful of all the movements on the extreme Right, build up an enormous machine by capitalizing the hardships of the unemployed and the frustrations of the lower middle-class. They were still unable to seize power, but they managed to make a farce of German democracy.

The only thing that could have checked their progress was a united front of the two workers' parties. Though the Communist Party made repeated proposals to this effect, the social-democrats, fearing that this was merely a man-œuvre to enable the communists—whose errors were certainly inexcusable in the dangerous situation—to secure control of the whole working-class movement, would have nothing to do with the idea. The mutual recriminations which came after the Nazis had taken power testify to the mistakes made by both wings of the labour movement. As the communists were to admit at the 1935 congress of the Comintern, they sought a united front *only from below*, and had taken too sharp a line against the socialist leaders—a mistake that stemmed from the overall Comintern strategy for Europe and from an underestimation of the loyalty of the socialist rank-and-file to its leaders and the strength of the joint fascist-nationalist revival. Socialists, however, saw that they reaped the fruits of their failure to break German reaction when they had the chance at the end of the war; they had left the capitalists and landlords in undisputed possession of their property and their reward was to see the industrialists openly subsidizing the Nazis, the nationalists calling for the repudiation of the Treaty of Versailles and the rearmament of Germany, and all the reactionary parties insisting that they should acquiesce in the suppression of the communists and the militant trade union movement.

The Weimar Republic, on which the social-democrats had

pinned all their hopes, was already tottering when the world economic crisis of 1931 dealt it a death-blow. As the unemployment figures soared, so the Nazis and the Communist Party gained ground, each racing to inherit the collapsing régime. Riots and street fighting became a common occurrence. The Social-Democratic Party and the other Centre groups were slowly being ground to pieces between the two extremes. They had completely lost the initiative. It was by then too late to undo the errors of the previous ten years. If another revolutionary crisis developed, they had no hope of riding the storm as they had in 1918. They could counsel moderation, as they had done so often in the past, but their advice was unlikely to carry much weight. Parliamentary democracy had failed in Germany and the leaders of the Social-Democratic Party were tarred with its discredit. They had to meet the communist charge that they had once more betrayed the working-class, as they had during the war, by allying themselves with reactionary parties and defending, instead of eliminating, capitalism. In reply, the socialists insisted that the communists were most to blame for the disintegration of the republic, for they had consistently attacked the democratic institutions created at Weimar as a sham, kept the country in a continuous state of unrest and, by raising the spectre of the proletarian revolution, provoked the counter-revolution which now threatened. Wherever the responsibility actually rested, these recriminations were no defence against the skilful agitation of the Nazis, who exploited the division of the workers' movement to their own advantage.

The social-democrats and the liberals hesitated to take the emergency power needed to suppress the Nazis, lest they were accused of destroying the last remnants of the democracy they were struggling to keep alive. The communists alone, and themselves subject to police persecution, were not strong enough to forestall the Nazis. Some communist functionaries, moreover, were under the fatal delusion that if the Nazis came to power the workers who remained under social-democratic influence would at last realize the futility of reformism and would rally to the Communist Party, which would then lead a successful insurrection.

At the beginning of 1933 the Nazis were the strongest single party in the Reichstag, and Adolf Hitler was Chancellor. Seizing the excuse of an impending communist revolt—of which only they were able to see any evidence—the Nazis took complete power. First, they suppressed the Communist Party; the Social-Democratic Party and the free trade unions shortly suffered the same fate, though some social-democrats at first tried to save themselves by giving conditional support to Hitler's foreign policy. In a short time the once impressive German working-class movement was in ruins and its leaders were either on the run or in the new concentration camps set up by the Nazis. Between them the communists and socialists had polled more than twelve million votes at the last elections, yet when the crisis came in 1933 they were not able even to call a general strike, let alone organize armed resistance to the Nazis. Too many of the workers had been deceived by fascist propaganda into believing that the Nazis really intended to carry through the anti-capitalist revolution which the Social-Democratic Party had not attempted and the Communist Party had been unable to accomplish.

Shortly after Germany went fascist a parallel attack was launched on the Austrian socialists by Dollfuss. In spite of the heroic fight put up by the workers of Vienna, they, too, had left resistance too late. In crushing the Austrian Left, the clerical reactionaries opened the way for the annexation of their country by Germany four years later, in 1938.

Thus, throughout Central and Eastern Europe, where the democratic tradition had never been very strong, the reactionary social forces were steadily regaining the positions from which they had been driven immediately after 1918. Even before the great economic crisis of the 'Thirties they had made a striking recovery, but after the onset of the depression they went over to the offensive, and one after another the bastions of democracy began to fall.

There were a few countries, however, where events had not taken such an unhappy course. In Scandinavia, for instance, the socialist parties polled more votes with every election. They neither threatened violence themselves nor encountered it from their opponents. They had long ago rejected the Marxist doctrine of bitter class-war, believing that constitutional reform was both desirable and practicable in nations where the workers enjoyed a comparatively high standard of living, where there was no large class of wealthy and usurious capitalists, and where a high proportion of the population lived on the land. They also found that, on specific issues, they were on common ground with the other big parties. There was no furious opposition to the development of trade unions or of the co-operative movement: they were not alone in demanding free and efficient educational, medical and other social services; they had no desire to expropriate either landlords or capitalists in order merely to satisfy a dogmatic principle. In short, they worked as radical reformers.

They were the kind of socialist parties of which the Fabians and Bernstein had dreamed. Peaceful, respectable and painstaking in their attention to administrative detail, they justly took credit for their share in making the Scandinavian countries a model of healthy and progressive democracy in which both State control and private enterprise could find a place. The socialists had not been involved in the catastrophe of 1914–18, and they were thus able to combine pacifism with patriotism. They saw no reason to revile employers who ran their industries efficiently and treated their workers well. They did not bother much with agricultural questions, for there was no large rural proletariat clamouring for a division of the land, and the farmers themselves showed a preference for co-operative methods.

It was true that a completely socialist society was still a long way off, but the socialists saw no need to hurry. Their countries were prosperous economically and politically stable. Why should they risk all that had already been achieved by the hard work of two generations? Premature socialization would only antagonize many people who were willing to support a comprehensive programme of reform, but who did not wish to undermine a capitalist system which was both flexible and successful.

Due to the special conditions of the Scandinavian States, this policy of compromise and gradualism did not lead the socialist movement into serious difficulties. If no substantial advance was made towards the traditional goal of socialism, the Scandinavian socialist parties were at least able to deal effectively with social problems such as housing and unemployment.

Much the same sort of thing happened in Switzerland. Though the Belgian and Dutch social-democrats would have liked to follow a similar policy, it was not quite so easy for them. Both countries had large colonial empires and their economies were peculiarly responsive to fluctuations in world trade; in both there were considerable religious minorities, and the labour movement, as well as other parties, tended to divide along religious as much as social lines. In Belgium, especially, there was a continual undercurrent of industrial unrest, and it was not possible to dismiss the Marxist analysis of capitalism as totally irrelevant to the conditions of the Belgian working-class.

The Low Countries, perched on the fringes of France and Germany, also had to take account of what was happening to their bigger neighbours. As soon as the threat of a new war developed, the defence of their neutrality took priority over differences about domestic policy. Even if the social-democrats had managed to win a decisive electoral majority in either Holland or Belgium, it is doubtful whether they would have been able to do more than nationalize one or two industries and carry through a few reforms unless at least one important State in Europe had also gone over to a radical form of socialism. For they lived always in the shadow of events beyond their control.

Russia, with its immense resources, could risk isolation and hostility. A small nation, dependent upon the trade and friendship of great capitalist countries, was not entirely the master of its own destiny. The socialists had to wait and, with the exception of a minority on the extreme Left, they were not unduly dissatisfied with their progress.

In a large part of Europe the World War ended in chaos and revolutionary unheavals. Britain, however, emerged from the conflict with its economic system still intact, though weakened. In spite of the militancy displayed by a section of the workers, this industrial agitation never looked like a serious preparation for insurrection. But the war, all the same, had changed the face of British politics. The swing to the Left, so much more pronounced on the Continent, had broken the hold that the Liberal Party had hitherto possessed on progressive opinion in Britain. As the Labour Party, which had been the third and junior partner in the wartime Coalition Government, began to attract a majority of the workers and some of the middle-class, and, consequently, to take the place of the Liberals as the champion of steady constitutional reform, so the Right wing of the Liberal Party moved over to the Conservatives, who were much more capable of defending the interests of property against further encroachments.

At the same time, the long years of socialist propaganda had begun to bear fruit. The trade unions no longer objected to the party which their funds supported adopting a nominally socialist programme. Indeed, as we have seen, some of the unions had already come out openly for the overthrow of capitalism during the syndicalist agitation which had preceded the war. In 1918, when the Labour Party at last drafted a formal programme, *Labour and the New Social Order*, it was thereby committed to socialism, though the word appeared nowhere in the draft. Simultaneously, it was decided to admit individual members to the party and to form local branches in every possible constituency. Up to this point the party had consisted of members affiliated through a trade union or through one of the small socialist organizations. This reorganization completed, it was ready to make a bid for a majority in Parliament.

The Labour Party now stood squarely upon its own feet. But the socialism which it had made its official policy was still the brand supplied by the Fabian Society. Though the influence of the Marxists had increased as a result of the war and of the Russian revolution, they had formed themselves into a distinct Communist Party which was violently criticizing—and was, in turn, criticized by—the moderate socialists. It was impossible for two groups so bitterly opposed to live together, and before long the communists were driven right out of the Labour Party and there was no nucleus around which effective opposition to the reformist policy of MacDonald and his associates could crystallize. The latter had things all their own way in the party when they insisted that, whatever the situation might be in Europe, in Britain there was no reason to question the possibility of using the ordinary constitutional machinery for the gradual introduction of socialism. Indeed, Sidney Webb, the most prominent theoretician of the Fabians, coined the phrase "the inevitability of gradualness" to sum up the Labour Party's philosophy.

The Labour Party, in 1923, won just under two hundred seats and became the official Opposition. When, in the following January, the Tory Government was turned out by a combined vote of the Liberals and Labour, Ramsay MacDonald agreed to form a minority Labour administration with the support—but not the participation—of the Liberals. Though this Government had some things to its credit, notably John Wheatley's Housing Act and its treatment of the unemployed, it could not live. For nine months the MacDonald Cabinet was wholly dependent upon the goodwill of the Liberals, and when this was withdrawn it collapsed. At the election which followed the Conservatives capitalized on the "Red Scare" produced by the Zinoviev Letter and won more than four hundred seats. Labour representation fell to a hundred and fifty—though the total Labour vote rose by more than a million—while the Liberals were almost wiped out.

It was soon clear that this electoral defeat was but the prelude to a general attack upon the whole working-class movement. British capitalism was in an extremely difficult position. It had lost its old supremacy in the world market as a direct result of the war. It was saddled with debt and obsolete plant. It had failed to improve its technique to meet the challenge of new competitors. If it was to regain a large part of its losses it had somehow to reduce its costs. The most simple and obvious way to do this was to cripple the trade unions and thus check their wage demands. The industrial picture, indeed, was very dismal. The miners, who had hoped for the nationalization of the collieries after 1919, when the Sankey Commission recommended it by the chairman's casting vote, were engaged in a long guerilla struggle with their masters. In other industries there was a growing strike wave. And in every large town there were long queues of unemployed outside the labour exchanges.

By 1926 a crisis had been reached. The trade union move-ment decided that it would call a general strike in support of the miners. The trade union leaders, however, had very little idea of where this strike might lead, for they regarded the strike as a purely economic weapon. It was intended to be a demonstration of proletarian solidarity, and when it actually started in May it fulfilled this limited purpose effectively. But it was doomed to futility, once the British ruling-class decided to resist it to the bitter end, using force to suppress it if neces-sary, unless its leaders were prepared to carry things to the point of revolution. As soon as this was brought home to them they capitulated immediately, leaving the miners to their fate.

Peace had been secured, though at a high price. For the way was now open for the restrictive legislation, embodied in the Trades Disputes Act of 1927, which the employers desired. This Act, moreover, served a double aim. By altering the basis on which unions collected their political funds it struck a severe blow at the finances of the Labour Party—a handicap which remained until the Act was repealed after Labour's victory in 1945.

It is surprising that this experience did not produce any fundamental change in the attitude of the British socialists towards the State. On the one occasion when they had presented a major challenge to the rights and security of capitalist pro-perty, every possible instrument of coercion had been mobilized against them. Yet in the years after 1926 MacDonald and his colleagues showed no sign that they had learnt anything from the crisis. On the contrary, they kept their eyes fixed on the goal of office and never questioned the assumptions on which all their activities were based.

It would have been better for the Labour Party if it had taken stock of its position in the late 'Twenties. It might then have avoided a second fiasco. But neither the defeat of 1924, nor the General Strike, nor the fall in union membership from over eight to under four millions, between 1920 and 1929, produced any effective challenge to the policy pursued by MacDonald and his friends. MacDonald himself had been caught up in the confusion of his phrasemongering and had lost whatever sense of reality he had ever possessed. It is not surprising he led his party steadily towards disaster instead of socialism. For socialism, to him, had nothing to do with the struggle of the working-class against capitalism but was "the rise of social unity and growth towards organic wholeness", which could only succeed if the workers condemned the class-struggle.

When, early in 1929, Labour emerged from the elections as the largest party, though it was still in a minority in Parliament, MacDonald had no hesitation in repeating the disastrous experiment of 1924, accepting office without power by the grace of the Liberals. Apart from its failure to deal with unemployment effectively, which aroused serious criticism within the Labour Party, the Government carried through some respectable legislation, and it had a good record on foreign affairs, but its standing was never sure. Once the great economic depression started, it was helpless. It was not strong enough to undertake any substantial changes in the structure of British society, even if it had desired, and such changes could not, in any case, have been made in time to ward off the worst effects of the crisis. It was consequently driven into an attempt to hold together the stricken capitalist system to whose eventual abolition it was committed. In this task, naturally, it encountered the hostility and obstruction of the employers, who believed that their interests would be better served by their own representatives in the Conservative Party. MacDonald, who was in a panic, was persuaded without much difficulty to desert his party and without its prior knowledge he formed a new National Government. It is a measure of the suspicion with which he was by this time regarded by most of his party that he was able to carry no more than a handful of its members with him.

But loyalty to socialist principles did not save the Labour Party from an overwhelming rout at the elections which followed. By 1931 it had no more Members of Parliament than it had had in 1918. The Conservatives were firmly in the saddle again, and once the immediate crisis had been weathered they were able to devote themselves to bolstering up British industry and agriculture by extensive subsidies, and by the encouragement of monopolies. In the subsequent economy drive it was not only wages that were cut. Expenditure on all social services was drastically reduced. But though a new wave of militancy swept through the Labour movement—reinforced by the agitation of millions of unemployed—there was little the working-class could do. Its party was in the wilderness, and it was to remain there all through the critical years when capitalism all over the world was passing through its most critical phase and when the development of the fascist menace was raising new and complex problems for socialists everywhere.

CHAPTER XV

THE STRUGGLE AGAINST FASCISM

THE world economic crisis and the advent of fascism completely changed the outlook for the international socialist movement. In the golden days of 1929, when capitalism seemed to be making a good recovery from the chaos and stagnation that followed the war, the Marxist prediction of an inevitable crash was dismissed as a dogmatic jeremiad. After the experience of 1931 it was clear that the revival lacked substance and that the plight of capitalism was worse than ever. There was, however, no prospect of an immediate or total collapse. In some countries a temporary solution could be found by intensifying monopoly control of industry, by bolstering the export trade at the expense of the domestic consumer and, as far as possible, by a reduction of living standards. In others this process was carried to its logical conclusion by the installation of dictatorships which liquidated the workers' movement, regimented the economy of the nation, secured full employment by preparation for war, and had no scruples about using their strength in order to ensure the success of their economic imperialism. But the more desperately each capitalist country tried to consolidate its own position, the more it was brought up against the rivalry of the others.

Some of the formerly backward States, moreover, had begun to reach economic maturity and were no longer content to tag along in the wake of the bigger Powers. Even in the territories of the colonial empires there was a growing demand for independence, both political and economic.

Whatever transient stability capitalism might achieve, there was no one who could confidently assert, as had been the fashion before 1929, that its future was either safe or certain. There was, indeed, a growing realization that socialists had a good deal of the evidence on their side when they argued that the choice before industrial society was between a complete surrender to monopoly capitalism—which would almost certainly be accompanied by a shift towards a fascist political structure, with all that this would mean in further and greater economic crises, to say nothing of the danger of war—and the transition to a planned economy which could organize social resources in an attempt to secure a rising standard of life for the people. There were, of course, considerable differences in the socialist camp about the kind of planning required and how it was to be achieved.

But, even in the United States, the home of economic individualism in the twentieth century, the great depression had opened the way for Roosevelt's New Deal. In Russia, after the breathing-space of the New Economic Policy, the Bolsheviks had managed to carry through the collectivization of agriculture and two Five-Year Plans, which had effectively socialized the economy of the Soviet Union, creating for the first time a heavy industry in the country to act as the base for further advances and, if need be, as a source of supply for the Red Army. Whatever else was known or feared about the U.S.S.R., there were few people left in the outside world who still seriously believed that the system could not work, and that a reversion to some form of capitalism was inevitable. It was possible to dislike the Bolsheviks' methods, but nobody could deny that they were actually building a socialist society which worked and into the bargain were rapidly developing the Soviet Union—a sixth of the world— from a weak and backward peasant country into one of the foremost Powers. This fact alone was of tremendous psychological importance.

In 1917 the Russian communists had shown that the workers could win control of the State; since then they had given practical proof that there was no reason why their version of socialism, at least, should break down. Thus, at a time when the capitalist nations were running into serious difficulties, it was natural that the successes of the first socialist State, which was forging steadily ahead, should exercise an increasing influence upon the workers, the intellectuals and, to some extent, on the lower middle-class, which had suffered a good deal from the depression. The Russian solution of the problem of colonial and backward nationalities, moreover, had a striking impact upon the movements for liberation in the colonies still controlled by the imperialist countries, where there was little basis for gradualist socialism —owing to illiteracy and the absence of civil liberties—and where the younger nationalists as well as the declared communists made no secret of their sympathy for the one great State which consistently denounced all imperialism and proclaimed its faith in racial and national equality. Throughout the 'Thirties the Bolshevik star was rising, and this was reflected in the growth of the various communist organizations in many countries. Even in Britain. Marxism as a philosophy of life began to take some hold after the world economic crisis.

But these communist parties were no longer the vehement protagonists of revolution, nor did they spend their time in violent polemics against the moderate social-democrats. Through the 'Twenties there had been a fierce factional struggle inside the Soviet Union against Trotsky and his supporters. They had claimed that Stalin's insistence that socialism could be built in one country—especially if that one country were as vast and as rich potentially as the U.S.S.R.—was reversing an earlier Bolshevik conception that socialism could only be fully established in Russia if at least one or two important industrialized nations had followed the Bolshevik initiative.

From this theory of permanent revolution, as it was called, it followed that if the revolution had failed elsewhere, then what was being done in the Soviet Union could not, by hypothesis, be socialism. Trotsky and his associates, therefore, moved into open hostility towards the régime, and particularly towards Stalin and the group of communist leaders around him. It was not a personal fight for power: it was a basic difference of principle. Stalin did not believe in meddling with the affairs of other countries at a moment when there was not the remotest prospect of a proletarian revolution, for he was convinced that this would lead only to disaster for the local communists and possibly for the Soviet Union. He desired to make the U.S.S.R. as strong as he could against the danger of attack. At the same time he sought to make the new social system a success, hoping that the workers of other lands would come to realize its advantages.

Trotsky, it is fair to say, wanted to carry socialism abroad on the bayonets of the Red Army. Stalin believed that it could be done more effectively by example.

But, as the inner-party struggle developed, it also assumed the aspect of a fierce contest for leadership and control. Later it was followed by a series of purges inside Russia, whose extent it is still impossible accurately to gauge. These purges, directed at "Trotskyists", both "Right" and "Left" deviationists, recalcitrant peasants and ambitious military leaders, undoubtedly strengthened the régime's capacity to resist the Nazi invasion when it came, by removing centres of actual and potential disaffection within Soviet Russia. But they not only reflected Stalin's anxiety about internal and external security: they also antagonized many in the West who saw the Soviet régime passing into a stage of more rigid political direction—of, to use the oft-quoted parallel, "Thermidor" reaction. Though the purges may have been necessary, they were a high price to pay, both in the internal problems created and in their impact on world opinion.

From the advent of the Nazi régime Stalin feared that Russia might face the fascist threat alone, and he wanted to avoid that. If the other States, the capitalist democracies, which were menaced by the growth of fascism, were to co-operate in a common front against Germany, then there was no purpose to be served by waving the flag of revolution at them and thus strengthening the hands of the reactionaries who wished to line them up behind the Nazi coalition against socialism and democracy everywhere.

All this, naturally, was reflected in the tactics of the affiliated sections of the Comintern. Most of them had broken a Trotskyist minority of their own and had more or less settled down to the new and more moderate line. In a large part of Europe, communists and socialists were both working illegally, and were subject to similar persecution. If fascism was to be checked, there had also to be a joint struggle by all progressive groups in the countries where democratic institutions of any sort remained to defend the elementary liberties and to rally resistance against fascist aggression abroad and the allies of fascism at home. In foreign policy this meant that the U.S.S.R. had to enter into alliances and agreements with capitalist nations—in 1934 she entered the League of Nations—to accept and foster the idea of collective security, and to encourage the national sections of the Comintern to give conditional support to governments which were willing to offer the hand of friendship to Moscow. In domestic policy it meant that the communists would refrain from putting forward demands which would isolate them by arousing the hostility of everyone but the most radical elements among the workers. Their task was to draft a minimum programme of social reform, which they realized would do little to alter the essential nature of capitalism, as the basis upon which anti-fascist unity could be built.

The seal was set on this change by the Seventh World Congress of the Communist International in 1935. At this meeting, attended by communist leaders from all over the world, George Dimitrov, the Bulgarian communist who had become general secretary of the Comintern after his successful defiance of the Nazis at the Reichstag Fire Trial in 1933, laid down the guiding lines of the new policy. Calling upon all communists to throw every effort into the struggle against fascism, Dimitrov urged them to secure alliances with the social-democrats wherever they could, since only a united working-class movement could prevent a repetition of the German catastrophe in one place after another. Dimitrov insisted that it would be folly to raise the question of an immediate transition to socialism in most countries, on the grounds that the fascists were rapidly gaining the upper hand in Europe, and if they succeeded in destroying democracy there would be very little chance of the progressive movement saving anything at all from the ruin. Thus the People's Front was launched on the world.

Although, in the countries that had gone fascist, the socialists had suffered equally with their communist comrades, the Labour and Socialist International was slower than the Comintern to appreciate the changes wrought by the emergence of fascism. It was, moreover, a looser and less disciplined body, and it was unable quickly to rally its forces. The social-democrats were also extremely suspicious of the Comintern's new line, regarding this as merely another manœuvre to enable the communists to capture the leadership of the working-class.

In each country, as the Axis Powers grew stronger, there were attempts to form a People's Front, which were supported by liberals and by a section of the socialists, as well as by its original sponsors, the communists. But the old feuds died hard. In some places, particularly in Britain, the social-democratic leaders were in a sufficiently strong position to frustrate any general agreement. The two Internationals did actually negotiate about common action and issued one or two statements over their joint signatures, but that was as far as they went.

In certain cases, however, a People's Front was, in fact, formed. France was threatened by the new German danger across the Rhine, by an active and dangerous fascist conspiracy within, and by a serious economic crisis. Though, in the seventeen years after 1918, the Left had never been strong enough to secure a majority in the Chamber of Deputies and had been deadlocked by parliamentary politics, the formation of an electoral alliance between the socialists, the Radicals and the communists swept into power in 1936 a socialist and Radical coalition, which enjoyed communist support. At the same time the two national trade union bodies, one of which was non-political and the other led by the communists, fused into a united C.G.T. In 1934 France had seemed on the verge of a fascist coup; during 1936 the propertied French feared that the revolution was at hand. All over the country, in a series of great strikes, the workers occupied the factories and offices, refusing to evacuate them until their demands were granted.

This movement to the Left secured concessions, especially in social legislation, but French capitalism did not wait long before it staged a counter-attack. The banks and the financiers managed to engineer a currency crisis, and refused to take any steps to halt it until the Left agreed to moderate its social programme and to hand over the direction of the coalition to the Radical-Socialists. From that point the Left was the prisoner of its Radical allies. It could not risk driving the Radical-Socialists into the arms of the reactionaries. If there had not been an external fascist threat the French Left might have taken the risk of a head-on clash with the Right parties, but it realized there was a serious danger that these would form an open alliance with the Axis Powers, as they had already done in secret. Thus in the late 'Thirties there was a political deadlock in France, which neither side was quite strong enough to break.

By 1938 there was no doubt about the aggressive intentions of the fascist States. Abyssinia and Manchuria had fallen. Germany had absorbed Austria. All over Europe the extreme Right was acting as a fascist conspiracy against democracy. Even in France and Britain, where parliamentary politics were still unfettered, the Left was deadlocked and there were many in the conservative parties who were anxious to do a deal with Hitler that would turn his armies to the East, against the U.S.S.R. Although the surviving socialist and communist parties were growing steadily, this gain was offset by the speed at which a new war was approaching, and by the necessity for the Left to take up the task of defending capitalist democracy from the capitalists, who had no further use for it.

The successes of the French Popular Front were a gleam against a darkening sky. But even before the socialist advance had been checked in France the Left had to concentrate on a more serious situation that had developed in Spain. After the fall of the Spanish monarchy in 1931 the Socialist Party had become the strongest single party. In the elections of March 1936 a Spanish Popular Front had secured a sweeping victory. Though the Communist Party had little support at this time, and though the socialists did not even participate in the new Government, the prospect of agrarian and social reform terrified the Spanish ruling-class. In July the monarchist generals, with German and Italian backing, started the civil war that was to last three years. All over the world the progressive forces rallied to the cause of the legal Spanish Government, which was denied its right to secure military supplies abroad in spite of the obvious and powerful intervention of the fascist Powers on the side of General Franco. Volunteers from every part of the globe found their way to Spain to fight in the International Brigade; the trade unions and Left parties in the remaining democratic countries sent foodstuffs and medical supplies to the hard-pressed Republican Government. The Left, in France particularly, identified itself with the Spanish Popular Front, realizing that France would be in great danger if it was wedged between a fascist Germany and a fascist Spain, but it could give little effective help because it had to face sabotage and obstruction from the Right, and because of the widespread fear—much of it pacifist in origin—that, by aiding Spain, France would become involved in a general European war.

But everywhere the Spanish issue became the touchstone of political allegiance. In deciding on which side of the barricades they stood in the struggle between fascism and democracy, men were, in fact, choosing their positions in the greater conflict between capitalism and socialism. If fascism won, the outlook for human progress was dim indeed. If, however, it lost, the decadent capitalism it represented would be broken too, and the movement towards socialism immensely strengthened by the experience of the struggle and by the removal of the main barrier that now stood in its path—fascist dictatorship.

This was why the Spanish war was no ordinary battle between a government and rebels. It was the forerunner of the Second World War; it was the point where two rival social systems met and began their fight for mastery. This was why it was fought with such bitterness and why, for more than two years, it was a question of major importance in international politics. This, above all, was why the victory of the Republican Government was the paramount desire of all socialists and communists.

These events, of course, were reflected in the course of British politics. The leaders of the Labour Party were able to find good reasons for their moderate policy. They insisted that they could only win a majority if they continued to present themselves to the country as a safe and responsible alternative government which, on winning office, would not engage in a wholesale assault on capitalism but would advance gradually towards a socialist commonwealth by a series of reforms, none of which would frighten the timid floating vote, and each of which would appear desirable in itself as a means of alleviating poverty, inequality of opportunity and economic inefficiency. In foreign affairs they stood squarely behind the idea of collective security organized through the League of Nations, although they had to take account of the strong pacifist tradition inside the Labour Party, exemplified by George Lansbury, its loved and respected leader in the House of Commons. This pacifism, and the even more widespread suspicion that armaments were regarded as bolstering British imperialism, were a great handicap to those who urged a firmer stand in international affairs.

Though this cautious policy did not yield a very good dividend at the 1935 election, the deteriorating international situation provided the Labour leaders with a strong argument against the more pacific elements in the party, and at the same time they were able to steer clear of any association with the growing Communist Party, which they believed would be a serious embarrassment to them in their attempt to woo the middle-class vote. When the Spanish war started, the dominant leaders of the Labour Party tried to damp down the agitation for assistance to the republicans until joint action by the unions, local parties and co-operatives with the communists forced the party leadership to assume a more militant attitude towards the Chamberlain Government, and to give practical as well as moral support to the anti-fascists. By then it was too late to do anything effective.

In 1937 a new party programme was drafted, setting out the measures which a Labour Government would undertake on the morrow of victory at the polls, and discarding the sweeping socialist proposals of its predecessors in favour of limited and respectable reforms. The new leadership that had taken over after MacDonald's defection had passed through a radical phase in reaction against the futility of the MacDonald policy, but that was over in the late 'Thirties. Once more the party organizers had their eyes on electoral victory, which would be achieved by a moderate though comprehensive programme. This was set out in Mr. Attlee's *Labour Party in Perspective*, and it did not differ in substance from the platform of the Labour Party in 1945.

But the expected election never came. The Labour Party was not strong enough to overthrow the Chamberlain Government or even to push it into sincere support of collective resistance to further fascist aggression. It could do nothing but protest as crisis succeeded crisis. Before long it was evident that appeasement could not be prolonged indefinitely. The choice before Britain was either to stand and fight or to capitulate to fascism. Whichever alternative was chosen, the democratic and socialist movement was faced with a terrible struggle for sheer survival. The chance of halting fascism in time had been lost, and socialists had to throw all their resources into the last desperate bid to defend democracy. If they succeeded it would be time enough after the war to settle the future structure of society, according to the conditions then obtaining. If they failed, then the prospect of socialism had vanished for generations.

In the event, the struggle was both more bitter and protracted than anyone expected in 1939. As much as the conflict of 1914–18, it further weakened European capitalism, broke the ruling-classes of the occupied and fascist satellite countries after their initial collaboration with the Nazis, and accelerated the movement towards the Left. At first there was confusion in the working-class movement. The 1939 non-aggression treaty between Germany and the U.S.S.R. left the communists outside the Soviet Union in an embarrassing position. Up to 1939 they had been violent opponents of fascism. Now they were called upon to eat their own slogans and to crusade against and obstruct the anti-fascist war when it actually arrived. While an overwhelming majority of socialists endorsed the war from the outset, the communists argued that it was a contest between fascist Germany and the imperialist States of France and Britain, that the workers had nothing to gain by supporting such a struggle and that their chief aim should be to prevent the two groups of belligerents from uniting in a common crusade against Soviet Russia. The desire to keep war from the Russian borders was, in fact, the dominating motive of Soviet policy, and this motive lay behind the reversion of communists to "revolutionary defeatism" in this period. This change not only produced defections from the various communist parties, it also widened the gulf between the democratic socialists and the communists. For many social-democrats this was final proof that communist policy everywhere was subordinated to Russian interests and foreign policy.

But the period of the "phoney war", in which Britain and France prepared to fight against Russia and Germany at once, was soon over. France was occupied in 1940; at the same time the Chamberlain Government, whose anti-fascist sincerity was widely suspected, was replaced by the Churchill-Labour Coalition. As soon as the Nazis attacked Russia in 1941 the communists within and without Russia were prepared to revert to an all-out contest against European fascism.

By then everyone except a handful of pacifists had taken a stand. Illegal resistance grew in the occupied lands, in some cases under communist leadership, for the communists had the organizational methods and experience suitable for underground work. Other parties—though they developed their own resistance networks and played a leading role—had no such machinery prior to the Nazi occupation. The more the worst collaborators were revealed to be business men and the old corrupt politicians, the more the workers and sections of other classes moved to the Left, towards the socialists and communists. The latter also had the additional asset of sharing in the prestige of the Red Army. Their policy earlier in the war was, for the time being, forgotten or forgiven in the face of their sacrifices in the resistance movements.

All Europe was in ferment. It was clear that victory and liberation would find the basis of the old social and political structure gone for ever. After 1941 the working-class movement had an overriding aim: to defeat the Nazis. On its shoulders fell the main burden of this task. It was not confused nor divided, as it had been during the previous war. Its patriotism and its socialism could be fused into one immediate purpose, directed against one enemy and shared by millions in the occupied and the free countries.

Just as the war was leading inevitably to a social revolution in much of Europe—though this revolution was to take a different form from that which failed after 1918 and was to be more successful—so it was driving Britain steadily to the Left. As always during war, the hope of a better and more secure future inspired the masses of the people in their sufferings and labours. But this time, it seemed, there was a real chance that the dreams might come true in part. For there had been many years of steady socialist propaganda, and it was evident that capitalism had passed its prime; the people of Britain had been given a serious political education by the slump of 1931, by the Spanish civil war, by the attitude of the Conservative Government towards fascism abroad and democracy at home, and by developments during the war itself; above all, there existed in the Labour Party a political machine which could profit by this wave of radicalism and could offer itself as an alternative government, staffed by men who had been at the helm in the war, which had never been properly tested by a term of office with a majority behind it in Parliament. These were the main reasons why, in 1945, Labour was given its chance.

CHAPTER XVI

SOCIALISM IN A DIVIDED WORLD

ALL political compasses have been seriously affected by ten years of war and the succeeding international tension. Yet nothing is more urgent, in a world which seems to be drifting towards another conflict before the immense problems created by the last one have been settled, than an attempt to find new bearings. The socialist today has no simple solution to the crisis. It is too complex, too frustrating and often too painful to permit any easy decisions. The pioneer socialists, whether you take Marx or Keir Hardie, had a vision of a vast army of the disinherited, invincible if united, marching inexorably towards ultimate victory over a capitalist system which they believed to be both morally wrong and politically doomed. By loyalty to that cause they judged a man or a party. By aid or hindrance to that victory they judged a policy. Today, however, it is clear that the developing world crisis has intensified the traditional divisions on the Left. As we have seen in this book, the split between the moderate and more radical groups, though it has had many variations, goes far back into the history of socialist theory and movements. In our own time, the primary division is that between communism and social-democracy, which has become wider as each acquired greater responsibilities and strength and as the necessity to take sides for or against communism has become more urgent. What were once opposing tactics within the working-class movement have become antagonists on the level of international politics as well. As the rift between the U.S.S.R. and the United States increasingly divided the world into two power centres, social-democrats and communists appeared as partisans of different camps. The former, generally speaking, chose collaboration with American capitalist democracy against communism: the latter, insisting that social-democrats had never taken any decisive steps towards the defeat of capitalism and its replacement by genuine and effective socialism, argued that the Soviet

Union, the countries of Eastern Europe, the Chinese communists and the communist or radical nationalist movements throughout the world had inherited the traditional struggle for socialism and that the anti-communist nations, led by the United States, were making a desperate attempt to check its further advance. The democratic socialists denied this thesis, believing that the U.S. did not constitute an "imperialist menace" but, on the contrary, was the most powerful barrier to further communist expansion.

When the war ended it was reasonable to hope that the working unity which had been established in a common struggle would be continued in an effort jointly to repair the devastation, to promote economic recovery, to set Germany, Japan and Italy on a democratic path, to establish new agencies of international co-operation and to avoid, above all, another major conflict. Though there had been some wartime friction between the major Allies—and a considerable degree of mutual suspicion and anxiety about post-war aims—there was a real chance that Soviet Russia would, for the first time in peace, find it possible to collaborate with Britain, America and other members of the United Nations for these common objectives. Certainly, in these latter States, there was a fund of goodwill and a genuine desire on the part of the people to give such collaboration a fair and honest trial. No one doubted that it would require much patience and many compromises from all concerned, but it seemed the only reasonable and palatable assumption for a war-weary and economically-impoverished world to accept. With diplomatic unity, naturally, went unity in the world trade union movement and co-operation, especially in the countries formerly occupied by the Nazis, between all those who had resisted and worked for liberation. In the nations which had borne the heaviest impact of the war there had been a steady movement to the Left, and the idea of socialist planning as the sole effective instrument of reconstruction found support beyond the ranks of avowed socialist and communist supporters. In colonial areas, too, the nationalist movements had made rapid headway and most of these were in some degree socialist in character. Though the United States remained wedded to the system of private enterprise, the prospect of using the period of recovery as the initial stage of the transition to socialism in a number of countries seemed very bright. In Europe it was clear that only widespread State control and ownership could provide the resources and central direction required to restore industry and agriculture and supervise trade policies in the difficult years head. Indeed, socialists in the West were ready to suggest the creation of supra-national bodies to co-ordinate such common problems as transport, power supplies and even trade policy. Such hopes may have been utopian, but they were a logical expression of socialist ideas. On the international level agencies such as the Food and Agriculture Organization, the World Health Organization, and the various secretariats established by the United Nations seemed to offer a means whereby rational discussion of great "functional" issues could be achieved and satisfactory agreements reached, bringing some order into a world which had suffered from excessive and selfish nationalisms.

That was the spirit which seemed so hopeful in the brief post-war honeymoon period. At that time coalition governments had been set up in several countries, in which communists took a share proportionate to the strength they had shown in the first post-war elections. If suspicion of communist motives persisted—and it did—it was more than offset by the part that they had played in resistance movements, by the high prestige of the U.S.S.R., and by the knowledge that at that stage it would have been almost impossible to govern without them and highly dangerous to attempt to govern against them. While they remained in a minority in the West of Europe, and never quite succeeded in accomplishing the fusion which they sought with the Socialist parties, in spite of strong rank-and-file pressure for unity, they were more successful from the beginning in the countries occupied by the Red Army. In these the pattern was quite different. The nations of Western Europe, though they had suffered greatly, had strong political traditions which began to assert themselves more and more strongly as the months went by. The communists, accepted as partners in the task of reconstruction, were always excluded from the dominant role in the coalitions, though in this period they made considerable contributions to recovery, pursuing their then current policy of co-operation with all anti-fascists for the national welfare. They played the game in parliamentary politics to an extent which surprised even their most cynical critics. They had perforce to take a different line in the former Nazi satellite countries of East and South-East Europe, where the political conditions were very dissimilar.

In these countries, namely Hungary, Rumania and Bulgaria, the old ruling cliques had been chased out with the Nazis. The Red Army became the effective occupation authority and broadly-based coalition governments were set up. In these the Communist Parties, though then comparatively small, were a numerical minority but their members held key positions, chief among which they chose the Ministries of the Interior, which gave them control of security and police agencies. All of these nations have a predominantly peasant population, and the peasant parties were the strongest electorally in the first post-war years. The communists, however, were able to use their cabinet positions and the commanding position their part in the revolutionary upheavals had given them, both to increase their control of the governments and to split the other parties—in some cases by the arrest or driving into exile of their leaders, in others by setting up rival parties or factions sympathetic to the communists who assumed the name and functions of the peasant or middle-class parties which were not prepared to go along with the communist programme.

The communist explanation for this was two-fold. First, they said, these countries were able to move at once to the establishment of socialism, without an intervening period of bourgeois democracy (whose blessings, traditions of liberty and justice, they had never known in any case), and this transition demanded an intensive policy of industrialization and widespread land reform. Those who opposed this became enemies of progress and of the "people's democracies", as these States were now called. Secondly, these opponents, failing to obstruct the social revolution by normal political means at home, had, the communists charged, begun to intrigue with the West for support, acting as spies and centres of counter-revolution on behalf of defeated domestic reaction and Western imperialism. At the same time the governments of these three countries, both for obvious economic reasons, and to meet Soviet demands for war reparations, started to integrate their centrally-planned economies with the economy of the Soviet Union and of other nations in the Soviet sphere.

Of course the Soviet sphere extended beyond these three, but events took a slightly different shape in Yugoslavia, Poland and Czechoslovakia. In the first of these a communist government led by Marshal Tito had been set up after the long and bitter partisan struggle for the liberation of the country. Though the Tito régime seemed to be rigidly orthodox in its communism, supporting the Soviet Union diplomatically and, at home, pushing through rapidly a socialization programme, serious differences emerged between Moscow and Belgrade. Tito, the Russian communists declared to a surprised world, had become inflated with the successes of the partisan movement, had disagreed with the Soviet Union, had not permitted free discussion within the ranks of the Yugoslav Communist Party and had committed a whole series of crimes, ranging from the shadowing of Soviet officials by Yugoslav secret police to refusing to accept brotherly advice to change his ways. This breach, which was accompanied by economic pressure upon Yugoslavia, did not lessen the Yugoslav attacks upon "the American imperialists", or Yugoslav praise for the eminent Marxist leadership of Stalin. Yugoslavia remained a communist State internally, but a heretic and outcast from the fold of the formerly united communist movement.

This was undoubtedly the most significant split in communist ranks since the great Trotskyist rupture. Yet, unlike that, it was not followed by fierce faction fights within the ranks of other communist parties, though some of these parties had, in the course of 1948, to correct "right-wing" and "nationalist" deviation on the part of some of their members. Certainly, as communism grew in strength, great variations of policy were bound to arise, for the various communist parties were operating under a great variety of conditions. In China, for example, the military victories of the Chinese communists created immense administrative and political problems for them. Though they had long experience in governing the predominantly peasant areas they previously controlled, and had a remarkable record of success in abolishing the kind of corruption and exploitation which brought the Kuomintang to disaster, the scale and historical importance of their victories changed the pattern of power in the East as decisively as the October Revolution altered the course of Eastern history. The shift of most of China into the communist camp was bound to have immense results throughout Asia and in the relations between Asia and Europe. Clearly, the development of communism in China would be very different from its course in Poland or from communist policy in France. The problem, internationally, for the communist movement became how to keep the various parties more or less in step and yet permit them to have the flexibility required by local conditions.

In Poland and Czechoslovakia, both nations with some "Western" traditions, the establishment of extreme Left governments took some time. Poland first had a coalition formed from the Left and the Peasant Parties, the latter led by Mikolajczyk, who had returned from exile in Britain to co-operate with the groups which had formed a temporary government under the aegis of Russia. But Mikolajczyk eventually chose another exile, leaving the government in the hands of the United Workers' Party formed from the fusion of the socialists and communists, and a rump Peasant Party, "purged" of its more conservative and anti-Russian leaders. Czechoslovakia also was ruled by a coalition, given prestige and standing in the eyes of the West by the presence of the National Socialist (Liberal, in our terms) Eduard Benes as President, and Jan Masaryk, the son of the founder of the Czechoslovak State, as Foreign Minister. These two men sought to make their country a bridge between East and West, agreeing to rapid socialization but seeking to preserve the personal liberties accepted in the West. Until February 1948 it appeared that the attempt might succeed and that communists, liberals and socialists might collaborate on equal terms. But Czechoslovakia became a victim of the "cold war". In the "February Days" the communists assumed *de facto* control, the Left of the socialists and of the National Socialists siding with them, and Czechoslovakia moved abruptly into the communist group of countries. Jan Masaryk died mysteriously and Benes himself became mortally

sick soon afterwards, being succeeded as President by the
communist leader Gottwald.

All of Eastern Europe, with the exception of Finland, which
remained, after two defeats by Russia, resolutely anti-communist, was thus firmly under communist control by the end
of 1948. By one means or another the communists had taken
over the government. In fairness, however, it should be re-
marked that, in spite of these rapid and drastic political
developments, all of these countries had made quite remarkable
economic progress, managing to restore their industrial output
to pre-war levels and above. The socialism they practised was
much more radical and "tough" than Western social democracy,
and was not popular among all sections of the people. But it was,
without doubt, beginning to work with quite astonishing
effectiveness.

Over the whole of Europe the political development of
each country fitted into the general pattern of Great Power
relations. The split undoubtedly began on the international
level. As it grew it was reflected in growing estrangement
between those groups which were prepared to throw in their
lot with Soviet Russia and the communists and those which
took their stand with the non-communist Powers. The more
relations between Russia and the West worsened, the more the
communists felt driven to consolidate their hold in the countries where they were at an advantage and to maximize their
opposition where they were minorities. Naturally, this produced great tension, especially in Italy and France, both of
which were shaken by great strike waves under communist
leadership during the early part of 1948. After the introduction
of the Marshall Plan the communists decided to attack it as a
tool of American capitalism for increasing its hold over Europe
and as a means for solving the problems of the American
economy. This, in turn, widened the gulf between the communists and the socialists, since the latter threw their weight
wholeheartedly behind the idea of European economic co-
operation and collaboration with the U.S. The hope of united
working-class action faded as, on the domestic and international
levels, socialists and communists were driven into opposite
camps, the former accusing the communists of disruption, sub-

version and, where they were in power, of tyranny, the communists denouncing the socialists as allies of reaction who preferred to collaborate with capitalism at the expense of the workers they claimed to represent.

Nowhere was this division, which was accentuated by the formation, in 1947, of the Communist Information Bureau (Cominform) as a new directing centre for communist activity in Europe, more marked than in Germany. By 1948 Germany was divided into two major Zones. In the East, under Russian occupation, the social-democrats were banned and their members had been fused into the Socialist Unity Party, dominated by communist leadership. While this party held the key positions in the Russian Zone, the Zone was still under strict Soviet control and its resources were being directed to heavy reparations payments. The Unity Party continually denounced the British and Americans for dividing Germany and for permitting the revival of reaction in their Zones. Certainly the hope of ensuring that the reconstruction of Germany was carried through on socialist lines, which would provide adequate guarantees against a revival of German militarism and perhaps the only real means of repairing the physical and economic ravages of the war, was doomed to failure as long as the nation was so divided. As long as Germany remained divided, moreover, and as long as Great Power hostility existed, it was inevitable that each side should develop a German policy designed to offer the maximum advantage in the tactics of the "cold war" and the best position in the event of open conflict. This unhappy state of affairs most profited the German nationalists, who sought to play off the Great Powers against each other in the belief that a strong Germany would most easily be restored if the victorious Allies could be prevented from agreeing on a common policy designed to settle Germany as a peaceful and prosperous nation in Europe for the first time.

Thus, East of the Rhine, the post-war years had brought very considerable changes in the socialist perspective. There seemed little chance, at the end of 1948, that Germany would go socialist, or be able to secure the unity which effective socialism required. In the countries first Germany and then Russia had overrun in the course of the war, communist States definitely linked to the Soviet Union had come into being and were proceeding on much the same lines of policy. Democratic socialism, in the Western sense, no longer seemed a workable possibility in these States.

.   .   .   .   .

Since the United States now plays so large a role in world affairs it is pertinent to ask at this stage why it has as yet produced no really significant socialist movement, although it has powerful trade union federations and a strong liberal tradition. Since, moreover, one of the most fundamental differences between social-democrats and communists today is their disagreement about the aims and character of American capitalism—is it a reactionary imperialism, or is its willingness to assist European recovery due to its recognition of a common democratic way of life?—the presence or absence of strong progressive tendencies in America becomes a vital question.

There are many explanations for the failure of American trade unionists and socialists to create a labour party on the European model, and the problem is so complex that it cannot be discussed properly in a brief summary. But, historically, there are certain important factors which should be noted.

During the nineteenth century, when waves of European immigrants poured into the country, many socialists went too, and founded small organizations in the image of those which were being built in Europe. But they did not succeed in reaching out to the American workers *as a class*: too often, these socialists found support only among the foreign-born in the big industrial centres. The Socialist Party, now virtually defunct, had polled nearly a million votes in 1912 and 1920, but it declined rapidly and neither it nor the Communist Party has ever secured a mass following. In a nation where, until a generation ago, there was always free land and new opportunity to the West, and where great mobility in occupation and in residence was a commonplace, the under-privileged could always move on, seeking their fortune elsewhere. The scarcity of skilled, English-speaking labour, moreover, until recent years, drove a wedge between the immigrant poor and the labour "aristocracy" which, in other countries, frequently provided the leadership of the labour movement. These things, coupled with the popular belief, which has died very hard, that hard work was all that anyone required to get on in a society without rigid class divisions, prevented the formation of a militant and class-conscious proletariat, such as existed in Europe. American industry was expanding rapidly, too, and so harnessed the vast resources of the United States that, in spite of recurrent crises, it was able to deliver a steadily increasing volume of goods and services.

No one should underestimate the hold that the two major political parties possess. Each of them offers a place to all sections of the people, from the big industrialist to the farmer and the industrial worker, cementing their loyalty through the network of local political machines which live by their ability to keep the party voters in line by the rewards of the patronage system. The composition, even the political outlook, of these two parties varies from town to town and region to region, but they act as semi-official institutions through which the ebb and flow of public sentiment can be canalized and given effective expression. It is a task of the utmost difficulty for any new party to compete with them. There have been attempts to break into the territory they control, but all of these attempts have failed. The latest, the Progressive Party, led by Henry Wallace, supported by the communists and by such sections of the Left as were prepared to work with communists, accomplished a miracle of organization by managing, at the 1948 elections, to get on to the ballot in all but three States. No minority party had managed this before. But the most the new party could poll was a million votes—less than two per cent. of the total. Politically, American liberals and progressives have chosen to work through the existing parties—increasingly, since 1932, through the Democratic Party that Roosevelt's leadership made an agency of social reform and a friend of organized labour. By pressing for such progressive measures as laws guaranteeing trade union rights, government aid to farmers, the creation of such great social enterprises as the Tennessee Valley Authority, social services, housing projects and public ownership of hydro-electric generation, most liberals feel they can do more than by going out into the political wilderness and pressing for more radical demands through a minority party doomed for a long time to impotent criticism.

This is equally true of the American trade unions. The philosophy of "business unionism" to which they have been long committed, exemplified by Samuel Gompers, founder of the American Federation of Labour, accepts the existence and continuation of capitalist ownership as a fact, believing that trade unions should confine themselves to collective bargaining with the employers, a process in which the State should intervene only in order to secure fair and equal treatment for both parties. This attitude is broadly similar to that adopted by the British unions in the later part of the nineteenth century, when there was the greatest reluctance to accept the idea of an independent working-class party, let alone endorse the socialist indictment of an apparently successful capitalist system. Where the trade unions in the United States met bitter opposition— and they have, over the years, had to face industrial conflicts which resembled small-scale wars in ferocity and duration— they did not turn to politics in any large degree, preferring to meet the struggle largely on the industrial plane. Where they encountered depression, they met it as far as they could by traditional trade union measures, though the great collapse of the early 'Thirties, and the Roosevelt New Deal which tried to restore the economy, swung the majority of the wage-earners over to enthusiastic support of the Democrats. When the unions moved into politics, from 1936 onwards, especially the younger and more militant Congress of Industrial Organization, it was as auxiliaries of the Democratic Party, committed to the preservation of the advances made by labour under the New Deal. This was the case in the 1948 elections, when the greater part of organized labour refused to follow Wallace into a new political adventure and threw its strength behind the effort to defeat the Republican Party, which had sponsored legislation attacking organized labour and emasculating the social reform programme which Roosevelt had inaugurated and President Truman promised to continue.

Both organized labour and the majority of liberals found, to their surprise and pleasure, that they had helped to elect President Truman and a Democratic Congress, pledged to a more radical domestic programme than any Administration in American history. If this programme could be carried out they would feel well rewarded for their strategy of support for the Democratic Party. As far as foreign affairs were concerned, both parties were committed to the "bi-partisan" policy, which included a "tough" policy towards the Soviet Union, economic aid for Europe, rearmament and, as a corollary of the efforts being made to halt the expansion of communism abroad, strong pressure against communist activities within the United States, ranging from the arrest and trial of communist leaders to the defeat of communist factions inside the trade unions. American liberal and labour organizations support the basic features of this "bi-partisan" policy, thus placing themselves in almost the same position as the social-democrats of Europe. Neither group has much love for the more reactionary aspects of U.S. capitalism, as they see them exemplified in the Republican Party, but they do not believe that the picture painted by the communists, which shows the United States as dominated by that reaction, is true to life. They point, on the contrary, to the defeat of the protagonists of unfettered free enterprise and of the great corporations at the last elections. America, they insist, may be anti-communist, but that does not, by definition, transform the country into a virulent imperialist menace.

The communist argument, in reply, emphasizes the unstable nature of American capitalism, its liability to another economic crisis which, communists insist, can only be staved off by massive State spending on armaments and foreign aid, both of which serve as subsidies to private capitalism. The inner drives of this system must lead it to economic expansion, to the subordination of the national interests of other States to American interests, and to hostility towards communism everywhere, as the only remaining obstacle of importance to its quest for world domination.

The evidence for this argument, the communists suggest, can be found in the chain of American airbases encircling the U.S.S.R.; in American dependence upon the atomic bomb as an offensive weapon; in American support for the decaying Kuomintang regime in China, for the reactionary governments of Greece and Turkey and for the revival of monopoly capitalism in West Germany and Japan; in intervention in the political affairs of Italy; and in the repression, by America's European allies, of colonial liberation movements in Indonesia, Viet-Nam and elsewhere.

. . . .

When the British Labour Party received a majority in the House of Commons, at the General Election of 1945 it also received a mandate to implement by democratic means the most far-reaching social programme that any British government has ever attempted to legislate in five years of office. More, this programme was to be put through at a time when Great Britain was faced with an immense task of economic rehabilitation of the utmost importance, both to the British people and internationally. If the Labour Party succeeded in its attempt to combine the reorganization and restoration of the British economy with rapid social progress, it would be the first social-democratic party to win power and begin the transition to socialism by evolutionary methods in a Great Power. Success in those objectives became a vital test of the virility and capacities of democratic socialism. The Labour Party, which has always claimed that the variant of socialism which it has created in theory and in practice could reconcile personal liberty and economic planning in the interests of the people as a whole, set out to prove its case.

There were two main problems to be tackled. The first was the introduction of the measures outlined in its campaign programme *Let Us Face the Future*. The second was the restoration of Britain's trade position to a level well above any previous peak, by increasing production, by extending the range and volume of exports in order to meet the enormously increased cost of the foodstuffs and raw materials which are so vital to the economy of a nation which depends so largely upon its manufactures, and by reducing the great deficits incurred in purchases from the New World. These problems, of course, could not be kept in watertight compartments. Each was dependent upon the others' success. If either failed to any considerable degree the entire achievement of the Labour Government would be endangered.

The Labour Party's concept of a planned economy differed greatly from that current in Eastern Europe or the Soviet Union. In the first place it sought to establish central control over import and export trade—a control without which scarce foreign currencies might have been squandered on non-essentials and Britain would have been left without the means to pay for the basic commodities without which industry would slow to a stop, and the policy of full employment would end in dismal failure. Secondly, the Government established a system of licensing and priorities to ensure that materials in short supply were available to the most important industries. Such controls were indispensable if Labour's type of planning was to work, since more than four-fifths of the British economy would remain under private ownership even when Labour had carried out its declared nationalization programme. To secure proper co-ordination between the public and private sectors of the economy the Cabinet had to retain general overriding powers of direction. Part of these, too, were the policy of restricted home consumption (or "austerity"), which released goods for foreign sale and kept import requirements down, the Government's fiscal policy, and the highly-complicated arrangements—ranging from working parties to State financial aid for industries in need of capital—by which co-operation was secured between the Government and private enterprise. Thirdly, the Labour Party began to place certain basic industries and services under public ownership, arguing that these either required reorganization and new capital investment on a scale which only the State could undertake, or that they occupied a place in the national economy of such vital importance that they were most properly operated by the State.

There has been, however, no wholesale and indiscriminate socialization of industry and commerce. On the contrary, in the sector of the economy which has been left in private hands it has been the policy of the Labour Party to give whatever encouragement it could to increased output, higher productivity (the key to industrial efficiency) and fair and reasonable reward to private capital. Finally, it decisively rejected any radical ideas of expropriation or confiscation, awarding fairly generous compensation when industries have been taken over for public ownership. This whole programme is motivated by the Fabian philosophy of slow and steady advance towards the socialist commonwealth, achieved by parliamentary methods.

Economically it reflects the strong hold which Keynsian theories have upon British socialists today. If the earlier generation of socialists in this country preferred the classical economists to Marx, so their successors have been far more influenced by the ideas of Lord Keynes (who adapted and developed the classical economic theory to fit modern conditions) than by any Marxist notions. From Keynes they learnt a flexible technique—though Lord Keynes himself was no socialist—by which the State could play a decisive role in the behaviour of the economy without the need to place more than a limited part of it under direct public ownership.

The pattern which has been imposed upon nationalized industries and services, which range from coal to transport, varies slightly. But all of them have been placed under the control of public corporations, responsible to the appropriate Ministers, but quite divorced from the direct operation of Government departments. The British Broadcasting Corporation and the Port of London Authority provided the models, not the Post Office, thus leaving the industry with a complete and separate structure of its own over which the State retains a general jurisdiction. Some criticism has been made of these corporations, the critics arguing that they are too centralized to permit flexibility where it is needed on the lower levels and that inadequate attention has been paid to the traditional demand of the workers for some part in their management. Trade union leaders, it is true, have been appointed to the controlling Boards, but this still left a vague and largely unsatisfied demand for a greater measure of "workers' control", though there is far from general agreement about the meaning of this phrase or how far the idea it embodies should be carried. Undoubtedly one of the most important problems British socialism had still to solve after four years in office was how to give the ordinary worker a greater sense of participation in management and a fuller pride in ownership. Satisfactory labour relations in the industries concerned as well as increasing efficiency and output depend in an important degree on what solution can be found. On the successful operation of the nationalized industries, moreover, the whole effort to create a more productive economy now rests.

This matter of higher production is the key, furthermore, to any further advance in the British standard of life and the huge network of social services that have been established. A nation cannot afford a universal health service, an improved and expanded educational system, generous national insurance and an increased level of consumption of everyday goods, to say nothing of a large-scale housing programme and, in the face of a tense world situation, a much greater burden of military expenditure than ever was necessary before in peace, unless it produces more. The slices cut from the cake of national wealth cannot add up to more than the cake itself. An essential part, therefore, of a democratic socialist programme in Britain is the drive for an overall industrial output much larger than the best that had been achieved in the past, when Britain was still very prosperous, with large investments overseas and a strong trading position. Yet this increase has had to be sought in the aftermath of a ruinous war, with much of the overseas capital lost, with large parts of the Empire and Commonwealth moving towards economic and political independence. It follows from this that the leaders of British socialism, in the effort to carry through their programme of social reform, have had to devote their attention to questions of output above all else. It follows, too, that the aid which the United States offered to European recovery became a welcome and indispensable asset to the Government's struggle to get through the difficult process of post-war adjustment without, at the same time, sacrificing its proposals for internal reform or demanding efforts far greater than would have been feasible from the British people and denying them even the rewards for their toil which they have in fact received since 1945.

This is the Labour Party's case, and the Government has defended it against criticism from the Conservatives and from the extreme Left, which regarded American aid as the instrument by which a decaying British capitalist system was to be made the junior partner in a partnership with an expanding and dynamic American imperialism, and argued for closer trade relations with the U.S.S.R. as an alternative. The Labour Party has continually contended that it saw no such danger and that the communist charge was as false as the allegation that

social-democracy was not merely too tender to British capitalism but was actually acting as a stopgap to help British
imperialism through a difficult period. Though the Labour
Party believed its record to be genuinely socialist, it did not
choose to line up with the communist part of a divided world
on the grounds that socialist Britain and the communist nations
had more in common, economically speaking, than socialist
Britain and capitalist America. On the contrary, it has taken a
stand with the United States against what it considers to be a
greater menace to democracy—communist totalitarianism.
British socialism, the Labour Party contends, is not in any way
imperilled by the United States. On the contrary, the United
States has chosen to give powerful aid and encouragement to
European social-democracy as a Third Force, standing between
the systems of the two dominant Powers and endeavouring to
mark out a peaceful and democratic road to socialism.

.   .   .   .   .

It would be utopian to expect any early or easy settlement
of the issues raised by the increasing strength of the socialist and
communist challenge. They reach into every part of the world
today. Great nationalist movements, strongly influenced by
socialist and Marxist ideas, are on the move in Asia. Communism is already dominant in China. In the British Dominions,
South Africa excepted, there are powerful or growing social-
democratic movements. Even in the United States, though
events take a different shape, there is developing a definite
liberal tendency similar in outlook to European social-democracy. And against this background there stands the power of
communism, concentrated in the Soviet Union, but a force
whose adherents are dispersed throughout the world.

Both socialism and communism have come a long way in
their comparatively brief life. Barely two generations ago the
world appeared to be moving towards a period of prosperity
and liberal freedoms. Yet it has been twice torn by terrible
wars and we are still passing through great social upheavals.
The path to socialism has not proved as smooth or direct as
the pioneers believed. Many milestones have been passed;
there are many more ahead. For there is no end to this journey.

A SELECT BIBLIOGRAPHY

THERE is a very large number of books on different aspects of Socialist history and philosophy. Those suggested below are a selection of the more important or accessible titles. Many of them contain bibliographies, or guides to further reading.

The best of the books designed as a comprehensive textbook is *Social Economic Movements*, by Harry Laidler.

On the development of Socialism and the working-class movement in Britain, see:

Max Beer: *History of British Socialism.*

David Petegorsky: *Left-Wing Democracy in the English Civil War.*

G. D. H. Cole: *Life of Robert Owen.*

G. D. H. Cole: *Chartist Portraits.*

T. Rothstein: *From Chartism to Labourism.*

J. L. and Barbara Hammond: *The Age of the Chartists.*

H. M. Hyndman: *The Historical Basis of Socialism in England.*

G. B. Shaw (ed.): *Fabian Essays* (1889).

Edward R. Pease: *The History of the Fabian Society.*

Beatrice Webb: *Our Partnership.*

G. B. Shaw: *Early History of the Fabian Society* (a pamphlet).

G. D. H. Cole: *The World of Labour.*

G. D. H. Cole: *British Working-Class Politics, 1832–1914.*

N. Carpenter: *Guild Socialism.*

J. Ramsay MacDonald: *Socialism, Critical and Constructive.*

Hugh Dalton: *Practical Socialism for Britain.*

Clement Attlee: *The Labour Party in Perspective.*

Allen Hutt: *Post-War History of the British Working-Class.*

G. D. H. Cole: *Fabian Socialism.*

G. D. H. Cole: *Short History of the British Working-Class Movement, 1789–1937.*

J. Strachey: *A Programme for Progress.*

A. L. Rowse: *Mr. Keynes and the Labour Movement.*

R. H. Tawney: *The Acquisitive Society.*

R. H. Tawney: *Equality.*

The most informative and reliable book on the German Socialist movement, *Geschichte der Deutschen Sozial-Demokratie*, by Franz Mehring, is not available in an English translation. *Evolutionary Socialism*, by Eduard Bernstein, is the classic statement of the "revisionist" argument. A recent book, *Hammer or Anvil*, by

Evelyn Anderson contains a good deal of material on the post-1918 history of the German Socialist movement. *Rosa Luxemburg*, by Paul Frölich, deals with both the German and Polish movements from a standpoint sympathetic to the subject of the biography.

Apart from the original sources mentioned in the text of this volume, some useful books on French Socialism are:

H. J. Laski: *The Socialist Tradition in the French Revolution* (a Fabian pamphlet).

E. Dolléans: *Histoire du Mouvement Ouvrier*.

Louis Levine: *Syndicalism in France*.

Paul Louis: *Histoire du Socialisme Français*.

F. Ehrmann: *The French Labour Movement*.

Of the writings of Marx and Engels, the following are of particular importance:

K. Marx: *The Poverty of Philosophy*.

K. Marx: *Critique of the Gotha Programme*.

K. Marx: *The Civil War in France*.

K. Marx: *Capital*.

K. Marx and F. Engels: *The Communist Manifesto*.

F. Engels: *Anti-Dühring* (or the shorter version, *Socialism, Utopian and Scientific*).

F. Engels: *Ludwig Feuerbach*.

The best biographies of Marx and Engels are:

I. Berlin: *Karl Marx*.

Franz Mehring: *Karl Marx* (in English).

Gustav Meyer: *Friedrich Engels* (also in English).

There is also a new and interesting biography of Ferdinand Lassalle:

David Footman: *The Primrose Path*.

On Anarchism, see:

E. H. Carr: *Michael Bakunin*.

P. Kropotkin: *Mutual Aid*.

P. Kropotkin: *Memoirs*.

David Footman: *Red Prelude* (this deals with the Russian Narodniks).

Of the many books on Lenin and the Bolsheviks, the following is a short list:

Popov: *History of the Russian Social Democratic Party*.

Short History of the Communist Party of the Soviet Union (this is the official Russian textbook).

Marx-Engels Institute: *Lenin* (the official biography).

Krupskaya: *Memories of Lenin*.

John Reed: *Ten Days That Shook the World.*
A. Rosenberg: *A History of Bolshevism.*
Beatrice and Sidney Webb: *Soviet Communism.*
W. P. and Zelda Coates: *From Tsardom to the Stalin Constitution.*
L. Trotsky: *The Revolution Betrayed.*

Lenin's own writings are available in English in twelve volumes of his *Selected Works.* Three short books, published separately, are of particular importance: *State and Revolution, Left-Wing Communism, The Proletarian Revolution and the Renegade Kautsky.*

Of later Communist writings, the most essential books are:
J. Stalin: *Leninism.*
G. Dimitrov: *The United Front.*

Very little has been said of the American Labour movement in this volume. An early but standard book on this subject is the *History of Labour in the United States,* by John Commons. There is also a more modern though short account in *The American Labour Movement,* by Ernest Davies, though this is almost entirely confined to trade union matters. A description of the work of the Political Action Committee of the C.I.O. is contained in *The First Round,* by Joseph Gaer, which has not been published in Britain.

The Theory of the Labour Movement, by Selig Perlman, offers one theory to account for the character of American unionism. *History of American Socialism,* by Morris Hillquit, gives an official socialist version of events up to 1912. See also: *The American Democracy,* by Harold J. Laski.

A number of miscellaneous books should also be recommended. There is a recent discussion of Socialist doctrine by Professor Sir Alexander Gray, called *The Socialist Tradition,* which deals with selected thinkers from an academic and non-Socialist position. Other books are:
E. H. Carr: *The Romantic Exiles.*
Edmund Wilson: *To the Finland Station.*
Max Beer: *Fifty Years of International Socialism.*
Julius Braunthal: *In Search of the Millenium.*
Adolf Sturmthal: *The Tragedy of European Labour.*
J. Lee: *Socialism in New Zealand.*
J. Strachey: *Theory and Practice of Socialism.*
Bertrand Russell: *Roads to Freedom.*
Edgar Snow: *Red Star over China.*
Stuart Gelder: *The Chinese Communists.*
J. O. Hertzler: *A History of Utopian Thought.*
Lewis Mumford: *The Story of Utopias.*

Maurice Dobb: *Studies in the Development of Capitalism.*
    Some anti-Socialist or critical books are:
F. Hayek: *The Road to Serfdom.*
E. Schumpeter: *Capitalism, Socialism and Democracy.*
L. Mises: *Socialism.*
L. Mises: *Bureaucracy.*
J. Burnham: *The Managerial Revolution.*
F. Pigou: *Capitalism and Socialism.*
A. Zweig: *The Planning of Free Societies.*
N. Berdyayev: *The Origins of Russian Communism.*

INDEX

189